"There is a subversive holiness in scared to tell, and Blaine has mast over and over again. Don't miss the invitation in this book to understand the significance of your own scars and what to do with them."

Jeff Goins, bestselling author of *The Art of Work*

"Blaine Hogan has inspired me for many years with his unique way of seeing the world. In this book you'll find a blast of inspiration and a trusty guide to help you exit the cave and enter a world that is real and beautiful and vital."

Brad Montague, *New York Times* bestselling author and illustrator of *The Circles All around Us*, *Becoming Better Grownups*, and *Kid President's Guide to Being Awesome*

"Blaine Hogan's memoir is an intense, stunningly honest, and profoundly hopeful promise that telling the truth can set the heart free. His story is riveting, heartbreaking, and hilarious. This brilliantly written and transformational book will allure you to tell your truths. You'll find yourself stumbling into grace."

Dan B. Allender, PhD, professor of counseling psychology and founding president of The Allender Center at The Seattle School of Theology & Psychology

"*Exit the Cave* is hands down one of the most honest and human books I've read in a long, long time. The courage Blaine Hogan unveils on each page, the wisdom and humor embodied in each chapter, and the storytelling are masterful. An absolute must-read!"

Steve Carter, pastor and author of *The Thing beneath the Thing*

"There are few books that mirror the dynamism of the human experience. That hold your hand through pain and joy, raw wounds and raucous laughter, all at the same time. Blaine Hogan writes with an honesty and an imagery that will wake you up and remind you you're alive. *Exit the Cave* is a gift for our time."

Ashlee Eiland, colead pastor of Mars Hill Bible Church and author of *Human(kind)*

"Blaine Hogan is a master wordsmith. This gift is not only delightful for the brain but also soothing to the heart. Especially when speaking of the raw realities Hogan shares in these pages. His vulnerability when telling very personal stories appeals to every aspect of the creative soul. And boy, has he accrued a deep well of wisdom by walking through the fires of life! As a creative who has also had my fair share of wrestling through the journeys of inner healing, trauma resolution, and mental health recovery, I savor each word as true, good, wholesome food for the soul. I am better today, in art and heart, because I've read this book. What a way to challenge and inspire the artisan soul that resides within every one of us! To use our pain and our trek through it as fuel to create wonderful things is a great gift that we are beautifully reminded of in *Exit the Cave*."

Christine D'Clario, award-winning singer, songwriter, speaker, author, advocate, and philanthropist

"Hogan's book carves a brave way forward for the Christian imagination."

Sara Billups, faith and culture writer and author of *Orphaned Believers* (forthcoming)

"Honest. Brave. Moving. Blaine turns his scars into lanterns, giving us faithful guides out of our own dark caves."

Kevin "KB" Burgess, rapper, designer, and Dove Award–winning artist

"*Exit the Cave* is a wise, hilarious, and memorable journey of Blaine Hogan's search for better questions and truer answers. Blaine invites us to see that healing requires us to enter the cracks and confront the ghosts of our stories in order to shape our desired future. As a licensed mental health counselor, I've longed for a book like *Exit the Cave* to show others that managing self-destructive behaviors is not only ineffective, it distracts us from all the heartache and glory that our life stories reveal. I'm grateful for Blaine's book."

Jay Stringer, psychotherapist and author of *Unwanted*

"This book brought me comfort in the hours when I didn't realize how much I needed the warmth and honesty of Blaine's words. The truth revealed in these pages helps me grapple with my own truth. Blaine's honesty and storytelling transport you to a fireside chat that lets you know it's safe to be yourself. He lets you in and shows you that you are not alone. There is such grace, humor, and healing in this journey. Blaine Hogan will inspire you to have courage."

Nikia Phoenix, wellness creative, storyteller, and commercial actress

"A glance at the table of contents alone reveals Blaine Hogan's intimate familiarity with the underworld of his own psyche, as well as his deep faith that alongside his fears and shadows resides his greatest stores of love, creativity, and wholeness.

He writes clearly, passionately, and vulnerably. In the space he holds, you will meet him—and you may in fact meet yourself."

Audrey Assad, musician, producer, author, and mother

"*Exit the Cave* is a tender but fierce story of survival, reckoning, and healing. Blaine manages to somehow weave themes of acting, allegory, family, addiction, faith, and redemption into one beautifully written account of his own healing. It's a testament to the miraculous powers of the human spirit, creativity, and love. This is the kind of story that heals both individuals and families. I loved it."

Laura McKowen, *New York Times* bestselling author of *We Are the Luckiest*

"Blaine Hogan has given us a rare gift in this book. Through storytelling rather than sermonizing, Hogan shows us the power of blessing the parts of our stories that have remained cursed for far too long, and he somehow wields his welcome with such levity and humanness that you won't want to stop reading, even while wincing along with him at the pain of what he has lived through. *Exit the Cave* is everything I want my clients and friends to experience—a tender and wise welcome home to the glory and goodness of who they already are. This is a story that heals."

K. J. Ramsey, licensed professional counselor and author of *The Lord Is My Courage* and *This Too Shall Last*

EXIT THE CAVE

EXIT THE CAVE

EMBRACING A LIFE OF COURAGE, CREATIVITY, AND RADICAL IMAGINATION

BLAINE HOGAN

BakerBooks
a division of Baker Publishing Group
Grand Rapids, Michigan

Published by Baker Books
a division of Baker Publishing Group
PO Box 6287, Grand Rapids, MI 49516-6287
www.bakerbooks.com

Printed in the United States of America

Library of Congress Cataloging-in-Publication Data
Names: Hogan, Blaine, 1980– author.
Title: Exit the cave : embracing a life of courage, creativity, and radical imagination / Blaine Hogan.
Description: Grand Rapids, MI : Baker Books, a division of Baker Publishing Group, [2022]
Identifiers: LCCN 2022006492 | ISBN 9781540900036 (paperback) | ISBN 9781540902184 (casebound) | ISBN 9781493432868 (ebook)
Subjects: LCSH: Mental health—Religious aspects—Christianity. | Christianity—Psychology.
Classification: LCC BT732.4 .H64 2022 | DDC 248.8/6—dc23/eng/20220414
LC record available at https://lccn.loc.gov/2022006492

The poem on pages 215–16 was printed with permission from Many Rivers Press, www.david whyte.com. David Whyte, "To Break a Promise," *The Sea in You* and *Essentials* together with ©Many Rivers Press, Langley, WA USA

The poem on page 231 was printed with permission from Many Rivers Press, www.davidwhyte .com. David Whyte, "The Seven Streams," *River Flow* and *Essentials* together with ©Many Rivers Press, Langley, WA USA

Published in association with The Bindery Agency, www.TheBinderyAgency.com.

Baker Publishing Group publications use paper produced from sustainable forestry practices and post-consumer waste whenever possible.

22   23   24   25   26   27   28   7   6   5   4   3   2   1

For Margaret

Contents

Part Three   Where Are You Going?

What follows is my story. But is it a true story, you might ask. The story is true insofar as I'm able to recall the events. Of course, the thing about trauma is that it fractures time and space and, yes, sometimes even memory.

———————————————————

It is by going down into the abyss that we recover the treasures of life. Where you stumble, there lies your treasure.

Joseph Campbell

Let me sing to you now, about how people turn into other things.

Richard Powers

Introduction

Years ago, while I was still the creative director of a megachurch, I was invited to speak at a conference on the topic of creativity. My flight had gotten in late, which meant I was exhausted from the travel and very hungry. I checked in to the hotel. ID. Credit card. Standard stuff. I then asked if there was any place still serving food. The hotel's restaurant was closed, they told me, but there was a decent late-night BBQ place that delivered.

Because the hotel was hosting tomorrow's conference, the lobby was filled with rowdy conference goers, despite the late hour.

How did I know?

Lanyards.

You can spot them a mile away.

Even though I love people and love even more the pre-conference mingling thing, I was ready for a bit of solitude. I put my head down and made a beeline for the elevator, hoping to not get—

"Blaine! Blaine Hogan!"

—noticed.

"Dude!"

I responded in kind. "Dude! Hey! Yeah. Crazy. So good to see you too. *Really* late. Weather, I think. I'm excited too. Pretty decent party down here, huh? Ha. Good one! I'm the first speaker though, so don't stay up too late. Ha! Yep. Well, I'm gonna . . . you know. See you tomorrow!"

I made it to my room and soon thereafter had a very delicious dinner. BBQ in the South is always good.

Because I'm no idiot, I'd ordered extra sauce, but just as I was about to put my pajamas on, I noticed the leftover sauce was becoming a bit pungent. I wouldn't consider myself a highly sensitive person, but the smell started to overwhelm me. And I knew that a good night's sleep was not going to happen if I didn't remove the stench from my room.

I packaged up the leftovers, opened the door to the hallway, stepped out, and awkwardly knelt to place the food in the little alcove next to my room where housekeeping might easily grab it in the morning.

I stood up and turned back to my door—just in time for it to slam in my face.

Welp. This was a problem. You see, I didn't have my key. Or a shirt. Or my pajama bottoms. I was standing in only my underwear. And I realized I had some very big decisions to make. Quickly.

OK. Think. You're a smart person, Blaine. How do you get a key to your room without drawing attention to the fact that you're gallivanting around in your underwear in the hallway of the hotel where you'll be delivering the keynote talk the next morning?

This truly was a riddle that subtlety would not solve. I was on the fifth floor, and I walked to the elevators where I'd remembered seeing a hotel phone. I called the front desk.

"Hi. Yeah. I . . . uh . . . locked myself out of my room. Blaine Hogan. 502. Nope. No. I do not have the extra key on my person. I'm sorry—come down to the lobby? You can't have someone come up here? You need to identify me? Sure. Sure. That makes total sense. No, we wouldn't want that. Um. OK. I will be . . . right . . . down."

I called the elevator and prayed no one was in it.

Bong! The door cranked open. It was empty. Success.

I pressed the lobby button and began praying the elevator wouldn't stop before I got there.

Ding! Floor 4.

Ding! Floor 3.

Ding! Floor 2.

Bong!

The door opened, and three people walked in.

No! OK, Blaine, keep your head down. Act normal. Like you're European. Going for a late-night swim. At a hotel that doesn't have a pool.

I glanced up. Lanyards. *No!*

"Blaine? Blaine Hogan?"

"Hi. Uh, yep. Weird story. I locked myself out of my room. And so . . . here is me. Here I am."

It's possible that I've never felt more humiliated in my life. Finally, the elevator door opened to the lobby, which was even more crowded by now. *Dang, creative conference people really know how to party.*

Of course, we all know the well-worn advice to the speaker who is about to head out onstage: "Just picture everyone naked." But I'm quite certain that no one has ever told the audience to picture the *speaker* nearly nude, parading through the lobby at midnight the night before the conference.

Heads were turning. I had to respond before the questions began pouring in.

Too late.

"Hi! Hey there! Yep. Crazy. Locked myself out of my room. Nope. Didn't prop it open. Next time, though, for sure! Nope. No extra key. I mean, where would I . . . ?"

I finally stood at the front desk. Without pockets to hide my sweating hands, I put one on my hip and let the other casually rest by my side, as the kind lady on the night shift matched my face to my driver's license photo she'd saved on her computer.

"You're wearing a little more in this photo." She chuckled.

"Yeah. Well, it was winter when that was taken."

"One or two keys?"

"Thirty-five, please."

Clutching a tiny, hotel-branded envelope packed with two plastic key cards, I sauntered back the way I'd come. When the elevator door opened, I turned to the onlookers, who were still a bit in shock, and shouted, "See you in the morning! And if you leave your room, don't forget your keys!"

They applauded my efforts. In return, I bowed graciously and backed into the elevator.

The next morning I stepped onstage, fully clothed this time, as the following quote faded onto the black screen hanging above me:

We are fired into life by a madness that comes from our incompleteness.

Fr. Ronald Rolheiser, *Forgotten among the Lilies*[1]

From the podium, I squinted out at a sea of faces—some of whom had seen most of what my mama gave me—and took a deep breath. I was about to bare myself in a different kind of way. Less humiliating, I hoped. But more vulnerable, to be sure.

Maybe those conference attendees expected a three-step plan for making good content, or perhaps a foolproof process for creativity under enormous deadlines and pressure. I'd not intended a bait and switch, but something about standing in the lobby in my underwear the night before made me rethink everything I'd planned to say that morning. The audience hoped for my trade secrets. I offered them my story instead. And with it, how my understanding of creativity, imagination, and courage came not by making art but by hitting rock bottom.

The truth was my life had exploded. The things I'd thought would make me feel alive and ease the ache of my incompleteness had only invited me into a series of tiny deaths—a seemingly everlasting loop of hiding and self-betrayal. Sure, I'd made interesting art, but I'd also managed to make a mess of my life. Eventually, everything had unraveled. I'd lost all hope and couldn't find my way. I didn't have the practice or the vision. And that lack of imagination had almost killed me.

What I'd discovered as I crawled out of the cave of abuse and addiction was that creativity isn't simply about making beautiful, meaningful art. Creativity is about embracing the courage required to make—and continuously remake—a beautiful, meaningful life. Not by relying on magic or muse but by mining the raw material of my story. Along the way, I'd battled demons that tried to destroy me. I'd warred with a tumultuous history that seemed fixed and finite. I'd faced the myth and meaning of the stories that shaped me. And then I'd changed the one thing I thought I couldn't: my past. My reward for surviving this journey was a new future and a new understanding of creativity—a kind of creativity that saved my life.

I suppose that's the gift of rock bottom. The pain propels you into something new. If you let it. And telling the truth really does set you free. If you tell it.

And so, I took one last deep breath, then I told the crowd the stories I am about to tell you.

PART ONE

Welcome to the Cave

1

Blaine from Blaine

It was 1997 and I was a junior at Blaine High School in Blaine, Minnesota, when I heard a story that changed my life.

Quick time-out. Yes, you read that right. My name is Blaine. I lived in the city of Blaine. And I attended Blaine High School. Crazy thing is, I wasn't even named after the town. I was born on the frozen tundra of Fargo, North Dakota. As luck would have it, we moved to Blaine when I was four. Not because my parents wanted to locate me within eyesight of a water tower that bore my name but because there was a cheap duplex for sale in a blue-collar suburban neighborhood. I will say, however, that as the smallest kid in every class, looking out at my name written in giant print in the sky did do wonders for my self-confidence.

Flash forward to seventeen-year-old me sitting in the back of a required humanities class in one of those '70s accordion-partitioned classrooms. The kind made of tall metal panels covered in frayed waffle fabric to feign privacy between AP

Spanish and Theater 101. Of all the subjects I took in high school, the humanities captured me. Featuring myth and story dripping with meaning and drama, it all made a deep kind of sense to me. It felt as if those Greeks really understood what this pale, skinny Irish/Norwegian mutt with freckles, braces, and a bowl cut who was from the Land of Ten Thousand Lakes was going through.

The story that gripped me and changed me forever was Plato's "Allegory of the Cave."

The words lifted off the page, through my teacher's voice, transforming into a full-on cinematic opera in my mind. We'd studied the many interpretations and potential meanings the ancient allegory held. The political, philosophical, and artistic lenses all made sense to me. But something more powerful, almost holy, happened as I listened to a fable that would go on to frame my life. It became entirely mine, a parable that hooked its truthy teeth into me and wouldn't let go.

The story, artistic liberties notwithstanding, goes a little something like this: imagine a cave, ominous and foreboding. As we venture inside, disappearing into the dark, we stumble upon an unsettling scene. In the deepest grotto, we find a group of people. They aren't delighting in communal celebration or joy. Instead they are a sea of blank faces staring up at a cave wall. Prisoners. Bound one to another, on and on and on, extending until forever. Held with chains ensuring they can only ever look straight ahead.

Humans. Flesh and bone. Meant for full life yet captive in a cave. Their collective breath echoes off the walls. An unholy mist wafts past their faces and parts to reveal the object of their attention. Before them, a rush of light and dark smashes onto a stone screen. Their heads crane upward as shadows, stories high, scurry up the wall of rock only to disappear into the inky abyss.

Behind them, situated so they cannot view it, is the source of light: a large fire, a raging tempest of heat. Between the fire and the detainees is a second group of people whose job it is to take an object and walk it past the fire, casting shadows for the prisoners to see. All day, every day, the prisoners are transfixed by this never-ending shadow play, this treadmill of repeating things. Sometimes they can make out the image: a tree, a chair, a dog. Sometimes the images are obscured, transforming into a terrifying form.

To the prisoners, these shadows are reality. They know nothing else. Hundreds of thousands of eyes are collectively caught; stunned gazes of sameness stare into a sea of shadows meant to resemble the real things of the world.

After Plato sets this incredibly elaborate scene—the prisoners, the fire, the walkway, the shadows—he zeroes in, reminding us that most of us live our lives this way. Until now, we've only been aware of the group en masse. But, like any good story, it needs a main character—someone who wants something and must overcome an obstacle to get it.

The cave needs a hero, and we're about to meet him.

His gentle eyes are open wide, different from all the rest. Slowly, we zoom in. Though he is filled with the same collective malaise, something else shines in him. A close-up reveals his breath. Yes. Even his breath is peculiar, containing something we've not yet seen or felt. *Hope.*

And then it happens. For reasons unknown, the man is set free of his fetters. For the first time, he stands. Decades of dust fall from his body. For the first time, he turns his head. Stunned, he holds his hands to his face, blocking the brilliant light of the flaming blaze that licks the roof of the cave. Through his blurry gaze, he struggles to take it all in. The cave. The wall. The walkway. The objects. The fire. His fellow humans. The false reality—all he has ever known—fades away. Then, just beyond the fire, he notices something else: a tiny white dot in the distance. He is pushed. Pulled. Called. Compelled. He steadies himself with a deep breath and begins his journey toward it.

A tangle of fear and curiosity grips him as he stumbles farther and farther from the shadows, farther and farther from the fire, farther and farther from all he's ever known. A chill sets in. Every step toward the mystery ahead grows more and more painful. But there is no going back now. He keeps moving. His pace is deliberate; the dot is now a large circle of light that keeps growing. Finally, the brightness explodes into an opening. The sun sears, and his eyes struggle against its burning, white-hot brilliance. It pulls him out into a new life filled with beauty and truth, illuminating reality for the very first time.

At last, he is free to exit the cave.

Sitting in the back of the class, my hands flat on the Formica desktop, I felt my body buzz with recognition. I'd known what it was like to feel bound to something outside of my choosing. I'd known what it was like to watch shadows made by someone else dancing before me. I'd known what it was like to hope for something more and the terror that came with taking unknown steps toward new.

The bell rang, and the shadow shows vanished.

In a daze, I sat stunned as my friends walked past me and out of the room, seemingly unaffected by the tale we'd just been told. They gossiped about the upcoming Snow Days Dance and the hotly contested controversy raging over bringing dates from other schools. Our teacher followed behind, casually asking me to turn the lights off before I left. Alone, I gathered my copy of Plato's *Republic* and stood.

Although I was only seventeen, I had plenty of practice hiding in the darkness, watching shadows. I knew the sensation of being trapped. I was familiar with feeling bound to the stories of those around me. The heaviness of it all pulled at me, like chains I couldn't shake loose.

But the story awakened something else within me, something with which I had less practice. In the courageous hero who dared an escape, I saw someone I longed to be. Someone brave enough to face the searing heat of the unknown for the sake of freedom. Someone courageous enough to hope.

As this ancient allegory collided with my very real story, a monumental thought rushed through my high school frame: maybe the chaos, disappointment, and abuse hadn't doomed me for good. Even though I couldn't name it then, I'd just been launched on my life's greatest quest.

Like Plato's hero, I, too, yearned for a freedom I only imagined existed. I, too, wanted life. I, too, wanted to exit the cave.

2

Waking Up

Every good story begins with a problem. A character is going about their regular life when an obstacle emerges or a problem that must be faced appears. Without dissonance or disruption, nothing would ever happen. If Luke Skywalker had known his father, there would have been no journey. If Alice had not been curious, there would have been no excuse for her to venture near the rabbit hole in the first place.

There must be, as my friend Carlos says, "a disturbance." If not for this, the hero would never leave home and become who they are to become. If everything is A-OK, why risk it? Why leave?

Screenwriters call this the *inciting incident*. Addicts, if they're lucky, experience this in what's known as a *wake-up call*. It is a moment that catalyzes a giant shift in the life of a person or a character, a singular moment or a series of events that demands deliberate action. And if you dig deep enough, everyone's life has one.

Years after hearing Plato's tale for the first time, I experienced just such a life-altering wake-up call—an incident that would catalyze one heck of a shift.

———————————————

I was a year out of college and renting an apartment in Chicago with a college friend of mine. Both of us were trying to make it as actors.

At just twenty-four I'd been lucky enough to land some good roles in good shows at good theaters. I was making a living as a professional actor. And while life seemed to be moving up and to the right, I had a sense of uneasiness that I just couldn't shake.

It came in the form of a low, distant hum, like I was passing under an electrical wire after the rain and sensing the muted buzzing of danger above. This unease had been coursing through my veins for some time. And though I thought of it as deep and dormant, nowhere near the surface, it was closer than I thought. Little did I know that distant hum was about to undo me.

On a silent winter night, as I lay in bed, it arrived with an icy crash. It sounded at first like glass breaking. I stirred. Then— *Beep! Beep! Beep! Beep!* I sat up, straining my eyes to focus on the red glow of the clock.

Was it my alarm clock?

Nope.

Maybe my car alarm?

Nah.

Back to sleep I went.

The next morning, the sun was sparkling, reflecting off the Chicago snow. I loved mornings like these. It was 4 degrees, but the crispness of the air and the brightness of the daylight glinting off the snowdrifts made it feel like summer to me. This is what happens when you grow up in the Midwest. These are the lies we tell ourselves.

As I walked closer to my car, the sparkles seemed to intensify. Sparkle on top of sparkle. Glass on top of snow.

My stomach dropped.

It *had* been my car alarm.

I stared in disbelief.

"Hey, is that your car?" A bed-headed neighbor craned his neck as he leaned out of his doorway on the other side of the street. I'm pretty sure he was still in his boxers.

"Yeah."

"Someone broke in last night."

"I see that."

"I saw it happen. Some guy smashed the window and ran off with the stereo. I called the cops. They turned the alarm off. You didn't hear it?"

I pulled out my brick phone and called my budget insurance company. Turned out having the minimum amount of coverage to stay legal didn't translate into stellar customer service. And telling Linda on the other end of the line that I'd starred in that hilarious wedding commercial for them last year didn't seem to do me any favors either. I'd have to wait a few days before they could get someone to repair the glass—and no, it would not be covered under my "discount policy."

The sparkling snow had lost its romantic appeal. I felt sick.

I think I probably knew it was my alarm that went off that night. I hadn't been sleeping well lately, and I'd also been attempting to quell the anxiety that had been quietly gathering steam for years by consuming copious amounts of pornography. I'd been living in a fog, which cost me part of my ability to engage in my own real life. Even if I had been certain it was my car alarm, I wouldn't have had the energy to chase a criminal through the icy streets of Chicago over a dumpy car stereo.

At the time, I was playing the illustrious role of "Orphan" and "Artful Dodger Understudy" in a production of *Oliver!* at a musical theater just outside of the city. Since there wasn't anything more that could be done with my car, I called a fellow Orphan to come pick me up for that afternoon's matinee. I didn't have time to patch the window, so I left it. And that was that.

Or so I thought.

Later that night, I again awoke to the sound of shattering glass. But this time it wasn't my car window. There was no sparkling glass or shining snow. The sound was coming from inside the house. I was the one fracturing. I was the one breaking apart. Sharp shards threatened to pierce me from the inside out.

I stood. I paced. I tried to talk myself down. I listened to music. I curled up in a ball on the floor. The far-off din swirled itself into a cyclone searching for a way to escape my body. I couldn't contain it. I couldn't shake it. I couldn't sleep. I couldn't breathe. My anxiety swelled. My fear multiplied. The pressure came from all sides. I wasn't sure what was happening, and I was terrified.

The storm within ached and pulsed. The hum that, for years, had rumbled in the background was now front and center. No amount of deep breathing or prayer stopped the waves of angst that kept hurling themselves onto my chest.

The medical term for such an event is *panic attack.*

The Mayo Clinic reports that an average person may have one or two panic attacks in their entire lifetime.[1] This was my first. When it crashed down on me, I couldn't calm down, and soon I couldn't even catch my breath. I thrashed my head desperately, trying to wipe the crazy off my face. I felt like I was dying.

I sent a message to a friend who suggested I go to the emergency room. I pulled out my wallet and fumbled for the new health insurance card I'd recently gained through my eligibility in the Actor's Union. On the back, it read, "$0 co-pay for Emergency Room visits."

I could afford that.

I grabbed my coat and ran down to the street. It was 3:00 a.m. A heavy snow had started to fall, and the wind was starting to pick up. I hurried to buckle my seat belt and began to drive.

Wind and snow slapped my face.

My broken window.

I'd forgotten I hadn't patched it.

The faster I drove, the harder the snow blew into my face. Desperate for distraction, I reached for the stereo.

My stolen stereo.

From the outside looking in, this unfortunate situation was rather comical. Were this a comedy, the synopsis might have read: "A young man having a panic attack is forced to drive to the emergency room in a recently robbed car, through a snowstorm, which is also occurring inside his '99 Saturn; we watch through his broken window."

I walked myself into the ER and sat down in a wooden cubicle, where a nurse checked me in.

"So, what's going on?" she asked, clacking away on her keyboard.

The other thing I'd forgotten was that I was going to have to explain this to someone else. I had only thought through the drive to the ER, not what I might have to say when I got there.

"Um, well—I'm kind of freaking out," I offered.

"OK, so is something wrong? Did something happen? Are you hurt?"

Yes! I thought. *Something is wrong! It's 3:30 in the morning, I'm covered in snow, and I'm here because I might explode out of my skin. Can't you tell that by looking at me?*

Instead, I simply mumbled, "I'm not really sure. I'm just . . . I'm freaking out. It said, 'Zero dollars.' So, I came."

I felt lost in my own body. I wanted to scream.

As I sat on the crinkly white paper waiting for the doctor, I felt a hot tinge of shame. *What* am *I doing here?* When the doctor finally arrived, he asked the same questions as the nurse. I gave the same answers. And without much emotion, he told me I was having a panic attack and sent me home with two prescriptions, Lexapro and Ativan, and had me take the latter right then and there. Ativan is a mild sedative used to calm the nerves, and thanks to the tiniest of white pills, my drive back home was a little easier. The darkest part of the night had broken into day as the morning sun peeked above the skyline.

The swirling snow sparkled again as it floated past my face. I tried to enjoy the fun of driving in my own personal snow machine. And even though it was still snowing inside my car, thankfully the storm in my body had started to subside.

3

Turning Point

Filled with stucco duplexes and townhomes, the neighborhood I grew up in was a place where tough-skinned truck drivers, commuting schoolteachers, and graveyard-shift factory employees worked their way through life. Like many in our town, I grew up going to Mass most Sundays. I never had a hard time believing in God. I accepted that He cared for me and mostly agreed that God saved people in one form or another. I'd been told in church that God was "always with you." But I could never understand why He wasn't "with me" when it happened.

In the summer of my tenth year, I was sexually abused by two older boys in my neighborhood. Bewildered and ashamed, I went silent. Not knowing who to share this kind of information with, I hid my abuse from everyone around me.

My brother and I were the definition of latchkey kids. My alcoholic father was in and out of our house my whole life, and my mom, a brittle diabetic, mostly lived life as a single mom. The winds of routinely unsupervised time and the tremendous shame from that pivotal summer swirled me into a world of pornography and set me up for even more abuse in the future. Like most addicts who find themselves already invested in their drug of choice at a young age, I felt a confusing mix of shame and safety with every hit. I found security, even if it was always followed with fear and regret. If God couldn't protect me from the very worst of things, I reasoned, I was going to cocoon myself with the delightful sensations that came from hiding in the woods to look at boobs in magazines and finding late-night flashes of skin on '80s cable TV.

After my abuse, my doubts about a God who seemed separate from these complicated experiences slowly formed themselves into a troublesome thought: *Maybe this "God-with-me" stuff is all a lie.* That subversive notion made its way into my tiny heart like a heat-seeking missile, sent to obliterate hope.

God did not save me when I was ten, and God was not with me now at twenty-four as my life spun out of control.

The months following my panic attack were haunted by a growing sense of anxiety so nebulous that I could never seem to place its source. Trying to wrestle my dread into defined boxes, I obsessively attempted to pinpoint reasons or pluck causes out of the air, but the answers always eluded me.

Later that year I was diagnosed with generalized anxiety disorder—a diagnosis often given to those experiencing post-traumatic stress disorder. Abuse, I was told, was classified as "trauma." I was also told that what I was experiencing was normal, since anxiety often followed such events, even many years later. I'd been seeing therapists of one kind or another since I was a kid, and the one I was seeing this time explained that anxiety alone is rarely the cause of the problem, that it's almost always a symptom of something else buried deeper. It's the body's way of telling you something somewhere in the system is broken. It's an alarm. And, if listened to, it can save your life.

Any story worth its salt sends its main character on a quest soon after a wake-up call. And my story was no different.

The call to my personal quest began on a stunningly clear October day, nearly a full year after my winter ER visit. It was early evening, and I was heading toward downtown Chicago on the Kennedy Expressway to do a show at the Chicago Shakespeare Theater. This was everything I had worked toward for years. A month prior I had landed a small role on the first season of the FOX TV show *Prison Break*, and I was working in some of the best theaters in town. On paper, I was living my dream of making a living as an actor. But as I drove, something blew in through the still-broken window of my car (I'm a procrastinator, what can I say?) and lodged in my gut.

An unusual feeling.

A passing thought that didn't quite pass.

I wondered for the first time what truly lay beyond the storm of anxiety and compulsions that had settled inside me. I wondered if there really was a way out of this cave. And if so, I wondered how I would ever be able to find it.

4

Addicts

Any repair of our fractured world must start with individuals
who have the insight and courage to own their own shadow.

Robert A. Johnson

"If you're wanting my opinion, I'd say that this is an addiction."
Michael spoke with the kind of level calm that made me believe
this wasn't the first time he'd said this to someone.

"I'm an addict?"

"Yes. You are an addict."

I was just twenty-three, living in Indianapolis, and nearly
finished with my final semester of college.

I'd met Michael, a therapist, when he was volunteering at an
STD testing site near my campus six months prior. Those days,
I was nearing the prime of my acting out, compulsively indulg-
ing in pornography daily and seeking random hookups. Every
time, after the high wore off I was met with ferocious waves of

terror. I learned the hard way that when the soul is unable to tolerate the anxiety the body is causing, and the mind doesn't understand the source of these anxious symptoms, it will do everything in its power to assign a source. Those post-high, icy-vein feelings floating around me were without form, so my brain began giving them shape: *I'm about to die of some terrible sexually transmitted disease.* Again and again, that thought seized me.

The only way to quell that awful fear was to go get tested. Obsessively. Given that those feelings were so frequent, I knew all the places around town to get a rapid STD test. One day, during a particularly acute episode, I found that my usual spots were closed. Eventually I stumbled into a place I'd never been called Blue Flower Clinic, which I'd found online. I jotted down the MapQuest directions on the back of a White Castle receipt, got in my car, and drove there as fast as I could.

It was fall, and Blue Flower was situated on the edge of an old college campus. Gray, gothic-style buildings of brick and stone formed monoliths looming behind the bright red and orange leaves that had just started to turn. My anxiety had intensified as I drove, and once I'd parked, I nearly ran across the parking lot, desperate to stamp out the panic inside me. The air was crisp, scented with the musk of fallen leaves that crunched beneath my feet on the concrete steps. I hurried inside.

The sterile, isopropyl smell of the clinic smacked me when I entered. I filled out the usual paperwork with its series of invasive questions about potential drug use, number of partners, safety procedures used or not. It's slightly jarring when the way you've learned to survive, numb, and run from your pain is spelled out plainly with such precise, clinical questions on a medical survey.

I took the test, set my watch, and headed back outside to pass the twenty minutes it took for the solution in the vial to read the drop of blood I'd left on a matchstick of paper and determine my fate.

These moments of waiting brought with them the usual suspects of bargaining with the Big Guy Upstairs. Even though my faith was on its last leg, such times of crisis found me scrambling for anything or anyone that might make this feeling go away. Even God.

God, if I get a clean test, I will NEVER do this again.

God, if You spare me, I'll devote my life to Your service.

God, please. Oh, please.

The little boy in me was begging to be rescued. When my watch beeped, I rushed back inside. The kind old lady from the front led me into a back office and asked me to have a seat. Clutching the chair's molded plastic sides, my fingers wrapped underneath. As I was holding on to the chair for dear life, I noticed it was the same fiery-orange color as the leaves falling outside. Lost in a trance, I sighed and wished I was a leaf freely floating through the air without a care in the world. The door opened, snapping me back into the room, and in walked Michael—the counselor on call and the carrier of doom.

He smiled softly, and then he looked at his clipboard.

"You're negative," he said.

"Is that good or bad? I can never remember."

"In this case, negative is good."

I exhaled and closed my eyes. A tear quietly escaped, which I immediately wiped away. I took another deep breath and realized how tired I was.

Michael set down his clipboard. "Blaine, can I ask? How are you feeling?"

The wind outside picked up, turning the smattering of leaves resting on the stone sill into a tornado of red and orange. My whole life was starting to feel like the same kind of vicious cyclone.

I feel out of control.

I don't know if I can stop.

I don't know if I want to stop.

What happens if I can't stop?

Tears began to flow, quickly turning into deep sobs. Unable to share my shame with the other human in the room, I swung my face toward the ceiling. Everything seemed to pause. Shame. Fear. Grief. Jealousy. They all hung in the air around me.

The short-lived relief that I wasn't dying right then of some STD faded. I must have looked like someone who needed extra help, because Michael reached into his pocket and kindly whispered, "I'm not really supposed to do this."

Then he handed me his card.

Months later, as I sat in his therapy office, he spoke the four words that would define the journey before me.

"You are an addict."

As the words settled in, I looked over to my on-again, off-again girlfriend, Margaret, who'd come to the appointment with me. She needed to know the truth and hear those words for herself so that she could figure out what to make of me and our relationship. We'd met two years prior when I transferred to Butler University. She had been a sophomore in the theater program I'd just entered. She was whip smart, with magical blue-gray eyes that were as bright as they were discerning.

Our first date came by way of a dental accident. Margaret was in her sorority house, preparing for a night out with her roommates to go see early-2000s heartbreakers 'N Sync. Before they left, Margaret bit down on a tortilla chip, and as she did, she chomped down on a dental cap she'd had since a childhood mishap with a bed and a wooden dresser. Fearing that she was now chewing on more than a handful of chips, she curled her upper lip in the mirror, took a look at her pearly whites, and confirmed her suspicions. Her cap was gone and what remained could only be described as a fang. Knowing that she couldn't let Justin Timberlake see her in this condition, she gave up her ticket to pop-star bliss and called her mom, who immediately booked her a flight back to the suburbs of Chicago and an emergency dentist appointment.

There was just one problem. To make her flight the next day meant she'd have to miss an all-important audition for an acting class taught by the meanest and best instructor at our school: Trudie.

Her attitude toward skipping was not very gracious. "Unless you or a family member are dead, I will enjoy seeing you in my class every single day." She didn't mess around. Now technically, Margaret had a dead pirate tooth, which did seem like a reasonable excuse to miss just one class. However, she would have to call Trudie and beg for mercy. As she sat toothless at the sorority house, she brainstormed who on earth would have Trudie's home phone number. And then it hit her: that hotshot transfer student, who was always doing handstands in his tearaway Adidas pants and Capezio dance shoes.

Across campus, my phone rang. "Hello."

"Hey. It's Margaret."

"Oh. Hi. What's up?"

"Um, well. Uh. Do you have Trudie's phone number, by any chance?"

"I do."

Short pause.

"Can I *have* it?"

"Why do you need it?"

"I just do."

"Did someone die?"

Long pause.

"Not exactly."

Eventually I coaxed Margaret to tell me the whole story. Armed with all of the details, I saw an opportunity.

"OK, I'll give you her number."

"Thanks."

"On one condition."

"What is it?"

"Meet me at Starbucks."

"What? No. Just give me her number."

"I will give you her number if you meet me at Starbucks. I'm sure it's not that bad."

Twenty minutes later, in the corner of our crowded campus coffee shop, we sat awkwardly at a tiny table. We chatted over a vanilla latte and hot tea, and all the while Margaret held her hand up in front of her mouth. Eventually I relented and handed over Trudie's phone number. Those few silly moments ticked away, turning themselves into an all-night conversation where we shared (and overshared) our family histories, along with the ups and downs of living with addicted and recovering parents. While my house broke apart, hers was pulled together by the saving power of AA and Jesus Christ, who was introduced to her parents through a community of good people at a local evangelical megachurch back in Chicago, a church that would eventually become central to so much of our lives.

Having both come from homes marked by addiction, it only took a matter of months after our very weird first date to realize that the magnetic force of our codependence was too strong to keep us apart. Our relationship was sweet at times. Tragic at others. But this moment back in Michael's office was one of our worst.

"An addict?" I repeated the words slowly.

As I took in the gravity of the phrase, Margaret put her hand on mine and gripped it tight.

A strange sense of peace overwhelmed me. It was out there. It had been spoken. I had agreed. And there were witnesses. Miraculously, I didn't combust out of fear or shame. Instead, I was thankful to finally be invited into the truth.

I once heard Ian Morgan Cron, an author and recovering addict, make the following audacious claim: "We're all addicted to something." He went on to say that even if a person isn't into the perceived hard stuff like sex, drugs, or alcohol, we're all suffering from the affliction of addiction. Being addicted to something can mean a lot of things. Classically, addiction is anything you do or continue to do despite the negative consequences.

When we think of an addict, perhaps we visualize the drunk who crashes their car. The drug addict who overdoses. The compulsive eater who binges and purges. The workaholic who ruins their relationships with their children and spouse.

But in truth, if you don't have one of the "big" addictions, it just means that yours is more subversive. Your journey to rock bottom will look more like a subtle slide than a solid slam, because there are so many ways to be addicted.

We can be addicted to maintaining our appearance. We can be addicted to the media that constantly feeds us a never-ending supply of distraction. We can be addicted to unhealthy relationships, or we can be so addicted to the feeling of constant chaos that we self-sabotage anything that might create order and peace in our lives. Conversely, we can also be addicted to stability and security. We can be addicted to wealth, power, fame, or success. We can even be addicted to strict religious rules and formulas we believe will create certainty and control in our lives.

I continued to meet with Michael regularly that year. He taught me another way to describe addiction: "doing something to minimize or numb your pain." He helped me see that if a habit or mindset prevents you from experiencing all your feelings, if it numbs any parts of your insides, if it keeps you from being fully awake—look out. It's probably an addiction.

An addiction doesn't always cause outsized problems in your life. Instead, it might be doing something worse: keeping you asleep from the real life that's waiting for you.

From our earliest years, we begin to develop behaviors and rely on patterns of relating in order to deal with the pain and discomfort life deals us. These behaviors and patterns work beautifully when they are modeled and passed down from healthy, stable attachment figures, equipping and propelling us into a rich and whole story. But when they are born from dysfunction and brokenness, these behaviors can lead to ruin. To life stuck in a dark cave where the truth is obscured, where nothing changes and life shrinks.

Thankfully, my appointments with Michael reminded me there was light outside the cave. He pushed me to consider that I had the ability to make different choices, that perhaps I wasn't as stuck and helpless as I believed, that I carried within me the possibility of a different life. He sat with me while I attempted to believe in these new possibilities and wondered whether I had the courage to leave this known suffering behind for the unknown—a life I'd need new skills for and felt ill-equipped to lead. A life I honestly felt too exhausted to even contemplate.

It felt risky to move into the unknown. To truly move toward something new. I knew it would cost me. There were things I would have to leave behind. Things I didn't yet know how to live without. Crawling out from the darkness and into the light sounded exposing and offered a world of pain all its own. But somehow I knew it was better than looking at shadows for the rest of my life.

5

The Jacket

I stopped counting the times my dad came and went while I was growing up. His ins and outs always coincided with whether he was drinking again and whether my mom was in the mood to dole out second chances.

Once, when I was seventeen, the same year I discovered the cave, I went down the stairs of our split-level to look for a jacket to wear to the Snow Days Dance everyone had been talking about. My dad had recently moved back in, and this time his clothes had been jammed into one of the basement closets. The basement was next to the garage, and I wondered if the reason for this new clothing locale was to make his next move-out easier. Kind of like trying to grab the seat nearest the exit in case of emergency.

"This time will be different," was his consistent refrain.

I passed the bathroom with the leaky faucet at the end of the hall—the one the abuse occurred in, the one I stopped using the summer I turned ten. As I rounded the corner into the family room, I was struck by the familiar aromatic mixture of Old Spice, coffee, and cigarettes. It was my dad's custom to do a few rounds of sit-ups every morning down there. It was also his custom to sip from his souvenir-sized cup of steaming Folgers coffee with two ice cubes in it and take a drag from his Marlboro after every set. Even though it was now evening, his scent lingered. It always lingered.

I opened the closet door and sifted through his wares, thumbing the fabric textures. Thin, soft plastic bags clung to recently dry-cleaned items. A scratchy wool sweater with a cedarwood hanger poking through it. A pair of linen suit pants with a subtle pinstripe I could almost feel. A camel hair sport coat.

Jackpot.

I yanked it off its wire hanger, the weight of the jacket snapping the hanger from the rod and catapulting it past me and across the room. The heaviness of the coat made it perfect for a winter dance, and I imagined draping it over my date's shoulders when she told me she was cold. Slowly, I pulled it over my shoulders and stuck my arms through the sleeves. A good tailor will tell you that a properly fitting sport coat should allow your hand just enough room to curl itself up and touch the hem of the sleeve comfortably without also causing the sleeve to curl up with your hand.

My hand could not be seen at all.

I'd always been a small kid. I got it from my mom's side.

I was once given a brand-new shirt from a guy at my church who'd bought it from a very fancy store in China. It was too small for him, and he'd brought the shirt to church that day to see if I might like it. As he handed it to me, he exclaimed, "And so I thought to myself, 'Who is the smallest man I know?'"

He said this as we stood in an elevator full of people.

I was thirty-eight years old.

———————————

I was sad my dad's jacket didn't fit. This sadness was felt on multiple levels. Though I had attempted different sports throughout my scholastic career in order to connect with my dad, we were never going to bond over my size or athletic prowess. This clearly showed as the camel hair devoured my diminutive frame. I tried rolling up the sleeves, which only made the cuffs look like giant fabric ringlets hanging from my skinny wrists. I then tried shifting the whole thing back, as if slouching it off my shoulders would help keep the flaps from touching my knees. Instead, this made me look from the front like I was wearing a robe, and from the back the massive shoulder pads had transformed themselves into what could only be described as "fuzzy back breasts." I jerked the jacket back into place as if sheer force might magically snap it into the right size, and as I did, the sharp corner of a mysterious object poked my chest.

I opened the jacket and saw the outline of a square pushing against the khaki satin of the inside pocket. My dad kept tags on clothes for years after the return date, confident enough in his storytelling abilities to come up with a reason why the kid across the counter would need to make an exception and exchange the very old and obviously used item. In addition to drinking vodka, pulling one over on a store clerk was a favorite pastime.

On one truly horrifying weekend when I was twelve, he convinced the teenage clerk at our local video rental store that the VHS copy of Madonna's opus, *Material Girl,* had gone missing for over a year not because we'd forgotten to return it (which we had) but because his son with a serious learning disability had hidden it from him. I stood next to him speechless as he spun his tale, trying not to die of embarrassment and also unclear of how I was supposed to participate.

Famous for phrases like: "If it's their fault, make 'em pay. If it's your fault, make 'em pay twice," "Keep your head up," and "Do as I say, not as I do," my dad held some strong beliefs.

Through the pocket, I ran my finger along the edge of the tag that had been poking me. As my hand reached inside, it was met with a stack of them. Ten or so. I pulled them out.

Only they were not tags.

They were Polaroids.

Slowly, I thumbed through the stack.

Each one featured a woman in various stages of undress.

Each one was taken in a place I recognized: an apartment my dad had recently lived in. The living room. The bathroom. The bedroom I used at his place.

I'd found magazines and nude photos before. In the woods. In the dumpster. In my grandpa's garage. Next to the toilet in friends' homes, balancing on top of stacks of *Reader's Digest.*

But I'd never seen something so personal. Nothing so bespoke, taken in places I'd been, created by someone I knew.

If I'd later come to discover that anxiety felt like ice shooting through my veins, the pain that was building inside me at this point in my life seemed more like white-hot steam. I felt like I was sitting atop an enormous locomotive barreling through the night to an unknown destination, the boiling mist shooting from the chimney scalding and stinging me. As the train rushed along the tracks, ferociously on its mission, beads of sweat formed on my brow, collected behind my ears, and dripped down the back of my neck. My hot, wet skin scratched against the camel hair coat.

I put the stack back in the pocket after ensuring they were in the order I'd found them, like a white-gloved museum curator gently returning a historical artifact that just told you everything you ever needed to know. Dazed, I retrieved the hanger from the other side of the room and hung the jacket back up.

I should probably mention that the woman in these photos was not my mom.

"Why are you so angry with me all the time?" my dad yelled as we stood toe to toe in the kitchen.

He and I had been fighting a lot those days. His coming and going was taking its toll. One night we'd gotten into a physical altercation after I refused to unlock my door. He'd crashed through it, and my younger brother had called the police. I sat on the split-level stairs as a police officer sternly suggested I listen to my father.

"You only have one dad," he told me.

Thank God, I thought.

I'd go on to keep many secrets in my life, but finding those Polaroids was like being asked to keep a secret for someone else without ever really knowing it.

Every shadow we look at in the cave is a secret in image form. It wants you to keep the darkness to yourself. This works, of course, until it doesn't. Until the secrets come spilling out one way or the other.

"Why are you so angry with me all the time?" he yelled again.

My mom sat watching from the round wooden dining table we'd bought her one year for Mother's Day.

"You want to know why I'm so angry all the time?" I shouted back as I whirled around. I rushed out of the kitchen and barreled down the stairs to the basement.

Back in a flash, my face was flushed, and my hand was full.

Then, with all the pent-up angst my teenage self could muster, I answered the question I'd left rhetorically lingering in the kitchen. "*This.* This is why I'm so angry with you all the time!" I flung the stack of Polaroids onto the kitchen table. They scattered across the surface like I'd dumped out a bucket of pure, liquid shame. And as the tidal wave of images broke, one washed ashore, falling right in my mom's lap.

I'd gone and done it. I'd cracked the whole thing wide open, and it was spilling out everywhere.

"What is this?" my mom quietly uttered.

Her eyes met his.

The shame on the kitchen table had suddenly filled the room, and I wondered if we all might drown.

Up to his eyeballs in it, he quickly said, "I have no idea."

So confident in his lie. So utterly confident. And yet so caught. So utterly caught.

"I have no idea," he repeated.

Those words reverberated deep inside my soul, like I'd just been taught a song that would eventually become mine to sing.

Time had seemed to slow, but now it picked back up and sent us into warp speed. The shame filling the kitchen watermarked the counter and then the tops of the cabinets until it threatened to crack the ceiling. With a torrent of force, the humiliation came crashing to the floor in a rush of questions and rage from my mom.

The tempest pushed me down the hall to my bedroom, leaving my parents to drown in their own collective contempt. I rode the wave until it placed me at my desk. Ripping loose a sheet of notebook paper, I scribbled out, "If you're not gone when I come back, I'm leaving for good."

So dramatic. So theatrical. Exactly what any seventeen-year-old thespian would write in this scene. Or maybe it was closer to the log line of a mediocre student film: *Wayward son gives ultimatum to alcoholic father before heading out on his own. Will they make peace before it's too late?*

Melodramatic or not, the pencil lifted from the page, and I watched as the wave floated the note back to the kitchen. Another wave rose and ferried me behind it. The note turned right and I went left. And as I rounded the corner to head down the stairs, the water twisted me around just as time stopped once more. Through the melee still storming in the kitchen, my dad and I locked eyes.

He'd already aged beyond his years. Cracks of lines encircling his eyes shook with tears and the searing blessing of being fully known. But there was something else there that I couldn't quite name.

Was it an apology? Anger?

A *How could you?*

Was it a thank-you?

Was it kindness?

Was it grace?

Had he been humbled or simply humiliated?

And what did my eyes say to him?

Help me?

Don't let me go?

Stop me!?

Or was it more like . . . *Watch me?*

Watch me go and be just like you?

I sometimes wonder what passed from him to me in that moment. What invisible, generational sin of the father was handed to me? What cells passed through our bodies? Through our looks? What transaction took place in that moment? What did he put down that I picked up?

Whatever it was, I agreed with it. Whatever the mantle, I took it up. Whatever it was he offered me, I grabbed it, folded it just so, and slid it in my Velcro nylon wallet for safekeeping.

That night I left, drove my mom's tan Ford Taurus to Eau Claire, Wisconsin, to visit my girlfriend, and lost my virginity.

And when I came back . . .

He was gone.

6

Chloraseptic

People either love musicals or hate them.

I belong to the former camp. I love the songs. I love the dances. I love the elaborate set changes. I love the literal theater of it all.

But what has always enthralled me most about musicals is the forcing mechanism that causes the characters to sing in the first place. In a play, people speak. As emotions grow, their voices either increase in volume and they shout, or they whisper, hushing their tone to tell a secret or to show off how in control of a situation they are. While there's certainly melody involved in speaking during a play, musicals are entirely more dynamic.

When a musical character's emotions have pushed them to the limits of what the spoken word can offer, when they can no longer speak, they sing.

Like I was the star of my own original musical, my shadows, my addiction, and my utter exhaustion pushed me to the edge of what few words I had left, and I began belting out show tunes as if I knew them by heart, singing the song my dad had taught me.

As the years went on, my addiction kept pace with my pain. The episodes were more persistent, riskier. Days were lost in front of a screen. Entire nights vanished as I went searching for another hit. And along with it all came lies that left my lips so easily. Lies became lyrics wrapped around melodies.

I knew I was ruining relationships. Hurting my friends. Hurting Margaret. Hurting people I didn't even know. And hurting myself.

I knew, cognitively, that I was moving further away from who I wanted to be. Further away from myself. And yet the desire to escape the pain of where I'd come from propelled me. A hit would quell the storm inside for a time. But the hurt always returned. And when it did, it demanded more, leaving me to take the whole ugly song and dance again from the top.

Feel the pain.

Feed the beast.

Feel the pain.

Feed the beast.

And-a five, six, seven, eight!

There's this musical theater old wives' tale (yes, there are such things) about a young woman who was doing a musical revue on a cruise ship when she came down with a terrible case of laryngitis. Instead of going on vocal rest, like the ship doctor recommended, she coated her vocal cords with bottle after bottle of cherry Chloraseptic, a numbing agent for sore throats. After all, the show must go on.

Now, any good vocal coach will tell you that a singer or performer (or anyone, for that matter) should never numb their instrument. The reason you shouldn't numb your throat when it's sore is because, eventually, often without knowing it, you'll overuse it. The pain exists to tell you something. And if you keep numbing the pain, you're liable to cause irreparable damage.

So this young woman went back onstage, singing her heart out in front of a bunch of snow birds and spring breakers, just going for it as she reached for the final note of the show, and then . . .

Her vocal cords exploded.

Literally.

They catapulted themselves out of her body and blood splattered everywhere. The show was canceled. Refunds were given. Therapy was had by small children. And the young starlet never sang again.

This was how hard I wanted to sing my song of addiction and lies. It's the tune I was taught and it's what I knew. But what I didn't know at the time was that the pain was trying to tell me something. I just wanted to make it stop. If I knew that getting a hit could, in any small way, give me a sense of peace, even for just a moment, I'd do whatever it took to get that high.

Of course, deep down I wanted off. I wanted out. I wanted someone or something to tell me that everything was going to be OK, to hold me, to help me, but when you're in the deepest caverns of the cave, where it's pitch-black and silent, it can seem like there's nothing to return your echo but the shadows cast before you.

So I kept at it and did the only thing I knew how to do. I kept singing and singing and singing and singing. I thought maybe if I kept singing, I'd feel better. Or maybe the whole thing would finally come to some grand finale. If I sang the song my dad had taught me, maybe I could explode myself out of the mess I was making. Or the part of me that couldn't be deterred or derailed would at least be destroyed. Or maybe, if all else failed, I could explode and disappear into the shadows that seemed to be swallowing me whole.

This is the razor-thin edge addicts walk between delight and destruction. Between self-realization and self-sabotage. Between listening to what our bodies are telling us and leaving it all behind. Between caring for the pain that is trying to tell us something and simply numbing it until we don't feel anything at all.

Addicts don't like pain and will go to dangerous lengths to avoid feeling it. Of course, I had no idea then that the pain was not something to purge myself of but rather something to pay attention to. I didn't know that it was trying to alert me to the places in my story that needed care.

But I'm getting ahead of myself.

It was my twenty-first birthday, and Margaret was throwing me a big party. As you can probably guess, at this point we were already doing the on-again, off-again thing, and she was learning to see through my lies. Having come from her own family of addicts with their own trade secrets, and armed with her very own secret decoder ring, we were the perfect codependent pair.

That night, just before the party, my phone kept ringing with the well-wishes of friends and family. I wasn't in the mood to talk so I kept sending it to voicemail, and eventually I just turned it off. Addicts have this uncanny ability to destroy the very thing that seeks to save them. You see, I wasn't going to the party, or at least not on time.

Because instead of showing up for my own twenty-first birthday bash, instead of tending to the pain that had been building for so many years by allowing a good group of great friends to take delight in me, I decided to metaphorically down a case of Chloraseptic and gift myself an anonymous rendez-vous with some strangers.

When I finally turned my phone back on, a plethora of increasingly anxious and fearful texts were waiting for me.

Hey, birthday boy!

We don't want to start without you!

Where are you?

Are you close?

Are you OK???!!!!

I showed up to my party three hours late, and I was covered in car grease, which I'd self-applied to cover the lie that I'd be singing that evening, entitled, "My Phone Died, I Got a Flat Tire, and I Had to Fix It All by Myself."

While it could have been a country tune, it sounded more like the blues.

I bamboozled everyone at the party, and they all ran over to share their condolences mixed with their congratulations.

"Oh, man! On your birthday!?"

"What luck, right?!"

"Well, I'm glad you're safe!"

"To the birthday boy!"

The champagne flowed, but I knew Margaret hadn't fallen for it. I could see it in her eyes.

And.

She.

Knew.

I was hiding.

Turns out, for both of us, this would be our saving grace.

7

Cancer

Six months later, I had to upend my plans to do summer stock theater because I had failed my biology class. And in order to graduate, I was going to have to take the class again in summer school. My biology blunder meant I'd have to stay near enough to campus that I could retake the class.

One of the dance instructors advertised her soon-to-be vacant carriage house near the school, and I moved into it at the end of the school year, thinking it would give me some independence and space from campus life. Maybe some time alone would help, I thought. The small abode was tucked behind a mansion that sat on Meridian Street, a historic boulevard lined with giant homes built in the early 1900s. There was even a pool.

Around this time, I was occasionally getting calls from my dad. We'd been talking on and off now for a bit, attempting a relationship though it was still fraught with tension. He'd not entirely sobered up, was still drinking, and was even doing some pain pills, it seemed.

I couldn't make this correlation until much later in life, but his addiction cycle had become a trigger for my own. If he called me drunk, it created such familiar chaos inside me that his failure to stay sober became my own great excuse to act out. And the only way I seemed able to quiet the madness inside was to sing the song he'd taught me, only louder.

One night, as rain spat against the windows of my tiny shack, the phone rang. My dad had called to tell me that, at a recent doctor's appointment, he'd been diagnosed with cancer. He didn't have much time to talk, but he wanted me to know in case something happened unexpectedly. I sat at the kitchen table, my face resting against the cold panes of a window, watching streaks of rain glide past as we both cried. He was scared. I was too.

Later that week I sat alone in a classroom taking an exam on *Hamlet*. I'd missed the actual exam because of a matinee for a show I was doing downtown, and the professor had kindly given me the option to take it later.

I stared blankly at the page.

1. Who killed Hamlet's father?
   Is my dad going to die?

2. What "poison" killed Hamlet's father?
   Is my dad going to die??

3. Why was the killing of Hamlet's father so unjust?
   Is my dad going to die???

I tried to focus on the questions, but the buzz of my anxiety quickly grew. My vision became blurry. My heart rate increased. It wasn't long before I was in full-on panic mode.

I excused myself to go to the bathroom. I splashed some water on my face and tried to calm down. As I walked back toward the classroom, I stopped in the hall for a moment—just long enough to realize what I had to do. I bolted for the exit and did not return.

Later that night, Margaret came by the carriage house. She told me she'd gone to the classroom around the time I should've been wrapping up the test. The professor informed her that I'd gone to the bathroom and never come back. She mentioned to him the bit about my dad. She also arranged a retake of the test for me, but maybe instead of an exam she and I could perform a scene. This would not be the last time Margaret saved me.

A few weeks passed. It was early summer now, and it seemed I might finally pass biology. As night fell, so did the rain. The carriage house was dry enough, but it was nowhere near warm. Nothing like the cozy brick fortress of a mansion out front that sat guarding my tiny dwelling. Two older, retired folks lived inside. I can't remember their names. They were kind to rent to me, though, and had only two rules: (1) Don't park in the back. (2) No parties.

As it rained, I kicked my feet up to eat my Easy Mac while the shadowy flickers of my TV, tuned to the Trinity Broadcasting Network, danced across my dark room. The glowing blue-gray hues inside the carriage house contrasted nicely with the orangey comfort of the lights inside the mansion. And while I knew my deepest longing was for that kind of warm goodness and safety, I found more comfort in the coldness of my hidden home. For fun, I sometimes pretended I was an aloof outcast, a Howard Hughes–type figure who was the real owner of the estate but preferred instead to live in the guesthouse and was renting the stately six-bedroom home to two darling old people I'd met outside a nursing home. Even if it was imaginary, I liked having some sense of connection and control in my life. God, how I wanted some connection and control in my life. I turned my head just in time to see the wife turn off the last lamp upstairs, leaving me with my cheesy noodles, Benny Hinn, and the satisfaction of giving those two old sweethearts a lovely place in which to live out their last days.

I'd had a penchant for TBN since I'd started college. I originally began my collegiate career in St. Louis, where my best friend, Josh, and I had gotten reasonably good theater scholarships. We'd known each other since high school, and together had a little comedy show. We were in high demand our senior year, booking a handful of senior parties. And when we both got theater scholarships to the same school, we jumped at the chance of a "Josh and Blaine Do College" spin-off series.

It became clear once we were about a year in, however, that the scholarships we received were commensurate with the level of production value at the school. At one point, the school was so strapped for cash they were trading livestock for credits. Josh left after our freshman year, and it was about that time that I discovered TBN. For the uninitiated, TBN was a network that provided nonstop 24/7 Christian programming and included everything from sing-alongs to Bible teachings to sweaty Southern preachers begging you to "Sew a $10 seed of faith right now to reap the blessings heaven is waiting to rain down upon you!"

I was fascinated by it all. Moved, even.

Judge me if you like, but there was something about hearing those good ol' Gaither boys and girls belting out "It Is Well," along with their catalog of more theologically questionable songs, that calmed me and salved my lonely soul. I was drawn to the music. To the spectacle. To the theatrics. To the seemingly unending supply of Holy Ghost power available to knock out entire rows of human beings. And yes, even to the hope buried deep within the gold-leafed facade. Calling the old ladies on the 1-800 number to ask Jesus into my heart became another odd lifeline. How sweet they were to listen to this college kid cry his eyes out for a few minutes as he confessed Jesus Christ as his personal Lord and Savior—over and over and over.

———

Benny Hinn had just knocked out another row of willing participants one night when my phone rang.

"Blainer!"

This was short for "Blainer the Complainer," a nickname my dad gave me when I was a kid. He called my younger brother "Blake the Flake." I'm not sure exactly when we were bestowed such titles, and I never could tell which name was worse.

"Dad!"

I was glad to hear from him. I knew he'd had some appointments that week, and I was curious to hear the results.

I tended to disappear from the first ten to twenty seconds of every phone call with my dad. A better way to say it was that I was hypervigilant. In those opening moments of a call, I didn't listen to *what* he was saying but rather what he *wasn't*. I listened for what was behind the words, under the words, around the words. I listened to tell if he was drunk or not.

And tonight, he was.

My heart sank.

I'd naively thought that a cancer diagnosis might jolt him into a new sober reality.

Maybe this time would be different.

He began weeping. Sobbing, really. "Blaine, I'm sorry, Blaine. I'm just such a—" Fill in the blank with whatever degrading phrase you will. He was the king of self-contempt.

I was sitting at the same table where he'd told me of his diagnosis weeks before. On that first call he'd sounded scared but sober. Tonight he was drunk, though still scared, and something deeper seemed hidden in his voice.

I couldn't quite place it.

Somewhere along the way, I'd become a kind of sommelier for my dad's tones, gestures, and emotions. Kids of addicts are amazing at this party trick.

And yet, tonight I couldn't quite discern this vintage's tannin. I could tell there was something he wasn't telling me. Through his litany of self-pity, I kept listening. Hunting, really. Digging through the words, around the words, under the words. Until finally he let it come tumbling out.

"I don't have cancer," he said through his sobs. "I never did."

He tried to say more, but I couldn't hear it, as I slammed my phone down on the table and hung up. I raged. I turned over a chair. I grabbed my journal and scribbled some dribble about being duped again.

"When sorrows, like sea billows . . ."

I chucked the remote at David Penrod's long locks, just as he opened his mouth to belt a high note. The force of hitting the screen split the remote and batteries flung to the wayside as the TV fizzled to black.

Thunder cracked, shaking the ground.

Water pelted the window, like bullets threatening to break through. I stood and faced the glass, hoping the rain-like rockets would tear me to bits in the process.

This was certainly not the first time my dad had lied to me. I knew he'd pawned my alto saxophone in high school for booze, and it had not just been misplaced. I knew he'd crashed his car into the office of his workplace, and he had not been transferred unexpectedly to another job. And I knew that the women he was seen picking up on the side of the road months before his marriage to my mom weren't just "friends who needed rides home." I knew he was a liar. But this, somehow, seemed like the worst lie so far.

Spinning with fury, overwhelmed with pain, and filled with hot, contemptuous shame that I could have believed him again, I needed a hit.

So I opened my laptop and pulled up a website I'd seen on the back of a newspaper.

And then . . .

I called a stranger from the internet.

Someone I could pay.

I was careful to remind her not to park in the back.

8

Now or Never

A year after my biology makeup was complete, I graduated from Butler. Margaret and I decided to take a break from whatever strange dance we were doing, and I continued trying to make it as a professional actor. So off I went. From starring roles in sold-out shows to embarrassingly mediocre musical productions at dinner theaters in Florida to auditions for Broadway producers to TV shows—I was a vagabond, traveling from town to town, wherever the next gig would take me.

Like a shadow, my pain followed me through film studios in big cities to showboats in tiny towns. What started at age ten—or, maybe more accurately, even before I was born— began to feel like it would never release its grip. My senses were dulling, forcing me to take bigger hits just to stay awake. My eyes were bleary from the toll of finding my next high, and my life veered dangerously off the highways I was driving on from city to city. Even the rumble strips of fear caused by thinking I was dying of something I'd contracted along the way couldn't keep me awake. By the time I found my way to Chicago, at twenty-four, primed for the great panic attack of '04, I was falling asleep at the wheel, and I wasn't sure I cared.

But . . .

My body did.

My soul did.

My *life* did.

About halfway through the film *Jurassic Park*, Jeff Goldblum's character, Dr. Malcolm, shares the danger of thinking you have everything under control and all figured out. When everyone learns that the dinosaurs are having babies despite all being female, he utters one of his most famous lines by dropping this philosophical bomb: "Life finds a way."[1]

I'd nearly resigned myself to the fact that I was going to end up like my dad. It seemed it was the only future my past would allow. But even though *I* felt ready to throw in the towel, *life* did not. Over and over, whether I wanted it to or not, life kept asserting itself, gently reminding me, *There is more.*

Whether it was the story of the cave I'd heard in high school or my panic attack trying to shake my body awake or Michael offering me care or Margaret reminding me that I was not disqualified from being loved, grace kept putting the paddles to my broken heart, jump-starting it again and again.

And as my heart slowly came back online, something of a miracle began to form. The possibility of a new future called to me from a great distance. It wasn't much, just a dot of light piercing the darkness of the cave. But it was enough.

Dr. Malcolm was right.

Life was trying to find a way.
My life was trying to find a way.

My story had brought me to a precipice where it became clear something had to change. It was now or never. Either I could choose to try something new or I could face the consequences of continuing in my old ways. I'd seen how this story was going for my dad, and I knew I didn't want that. But I wasn't sure I knew how to change—or if I even could.

After a year of living in Chicago, I began driving out to the suburbs for weekly therapy sessions and started attending recovery groups in the basement of a megachurch. It just so happened that this was the same church Margaret grew up in and the same one where her parents had found their own healing years prior.

One Christmas break while Margaret and I were "dating," she invited me to visit. The northwestern suburbs of Chicago were an easy stopover as I traveled from Indianapolis to Blaine, Minnesota.

I'd been in church buildings. Several, in fact. But as I approached this brown brick behemoth where I was to meet Margaret, I felt like I was entering the campus of a corporation. *Mega* was an understatement.

It was snowing as we snuck in a back entrance and stumbled into the main auditorium, which was more like a theater. Slack-jawed, I watched as a cast of what felt like thousands rehearsed their upcoming Christmas nativity play. But instead of the terry cloth, DIY depictions of Jesus's birth I grew up watching and participating in as Joseph or a donkey, this was more like a Broadway show. There were lights. A band. Projections. Production. I was confused. But mostly I was moved.

———————————

I started attending services a little at a time. I got involved in the department that put on the plays. I met people who saw me, who invited me, who encouraged me, and who let me serve while I was working out my recovery in those weekly basement meetings. It was good for me. The basement wasn't fancy like the rest of the joint, and frankly, I was just grateful to find that recovery groups at megachurches still offered cold metal chairs and served bad coffee.

As I started "doing my work," I began to read fare different from the acting theory tomes I was used to. I devoured authors like Anne Lamott, Frederick Buechner, Brennan Manning, and Ian Morgan Cron. A pattern emerged, as it seemed the only books I was interested in were written by addicts-turned-authors, or the other way around, depending on the tale they told. Each wrote with such clarity and conviction about the messiness of waking up, staying sober, and attempting to let grace have its way. I couldn't get enough.

At the time, I lived in Logan Square, just a few miles from Lake Michigan, and frequented the neighborhood Starbucks. Most often I could be found there memorizing lines or looking for temp jobs as I siphoned the free Wi-Fi. But that season saw me seated in a corner buried in a pile of very questionable reading for a person still doubting his faith (and his life in general), furiously underlining anything that spoke to me.

Somewhere during that juncture, a wise and kind friend named Tari suggested that I investigate the work of Dr. Dan Allender, an author, therapist, and pastor type. While he diverged from my usual library of addicts-turned-authors, he'd treated a lot of them. He'd also written the landmark book for victims of childhood sexual abuse, *The Wounded Heart*, and started a small seminary called Mars Hill Graduate School, which was later renamed the Seattle School for Theology and Psychology.

Want to know how to tell if someone is reading something they are embarrassed of? Look for the cover, or rather the lack thereof. Hardback—no jacket. Paperback—always folded over. Whether it's a steamy romance novel with some Fabio-like figure glistening atop a mighty steed or *The Dating Playbook for Men*, they are either embarrassed they are reading it or embarrassed for needing it. And I certainly didn't want anyone to see I was reading a book with the subtitle: *Hope for Adult Victims of Childhood Sexual Abuse*, which is why I simply ripped the cover right off. But while huddled in that corner of a Starbucks, having come to the edge of myself, the text cut deep.

Dan wrote,

> To the degree that we labor to keep ourselves intact, we become less human, less loving, and more like those who cavalierly abuse and dehumanize for their own survival. The honest person will admit that even though her fire-lighting strategies have won her a certain sense of safety, she is not living as she was created to live, and in the hollow chambers of her heart she is lonely as hell.[2]

The best path is through the valley of the shadow of death. . . . The journey involves bringing our wounded heart before God, a heart that is full of rage, overwhelmed with doubt, bloodied but unbroken, rebellious, stained, and lonely.[3]

I underlined in that book until I ran out of ink.

I'd crashed and was most certainly burning; my strategies were no longer working, and I was absolutely lonely as hell.

But God (whoever You are), I thought, *please no, not seminary.*

When I was growing up Catholic, the main reason I hesitated to go headfirst into religion, or even try my hand at carrying the thuribles as an altar boy, was because I was deathly afraid I'd be asked, through some mysterious calling, to become a priest. Even at age thirteen, I couldn't imagine never being able to have sex. *What would be the price I'd have to pay now were I to willingly enter a school that literally prepared people to become priests and ministers?* I wondered.

Also, what would become of the art I was making? What about all the art I dreamed of making in the future? I couldn't fathom a workable integration. To his credit, Father Reiser, my priest during my childhood, never asked me to smash my Aerosmith CDs like I'd heard my evangelical friends had to do. But would I be forced to do so now? While the Catholic Church had hired the greatest artists of the day to paint its cathedrals, the art I'd seen from modern evangelical Christians at its very best was poor and at its worst was propaganda. "Christian" or "sacred" art always smacked of cheese and fluff. I'd watched a lot of TBN; I knew my stuff.

And yet I was drawn.

Pushed.

Pulled.

I'd later come to understand that this provocation, this grav-ity drawing me into an unfamiliar orbit, was the Holy Spirit. And even though I hated the thought of abandoning the life I was building on the stage and screen, after countless anxi-ety attacks, pill bottles, confessions, counseling sessions, and consequences, I knew that following my ambivalence into the unknown might be the only way out of the cave.

Reluctantly, I applied to the Seattle School for Theology and Psychology.

Shockingly, I was accepted.

Cautiously, I enrolled and started packing.

I called my agent and said I would be moving and was taking two years off from acting to "figure it out." While he blessed my efforts, he didn't quite understand. I didn't really either. But that no longer mattered. Just two years after my car robbery and ER trip, I found myself in my car again. The back seat and trunk of my '99 Saturn were jammed with everything I owned. The window had finally been repaired, the stereo was new, and Margaret was beside me. For four days, we drove from Chicago to Seattle. It was the absolute definition of an odyssey. The log line of this new story might have read: *A young man leaves home to battle his demons in an arena teetering on the edge of Puget Sound. With his beloved by his side, he heads west in search of healing and hope.*

Throughout the tumult of my beginning recovery, Margaret began doing therapy work of her own. Slowly, as we began to understand some of the unhealthy patterns born prior to us meeting that made us so irresistible to one another, we wanted to see if there was something outside of the intensity of soaring highs and dangerous lows. We continued working on ourselves and our relationship, but boy was it messy. We approached the idea of me being away for so long and held it all with open hands, leaving our relationship at a "we'll-see-what-this-place-does-to-us-maybe-let's-try-long-distance" status, sensing that whatever might happen next would either break us apart or bind us together for good. The truth is, neither of us knew who we would be on the other side of this quest. We both tried our best to be brave and to hold this unfolding season loosely. After a long trek across the country together, Margaret left me and my car at a house full of guys I'd never met and flew back to Chicago. The trails of grace she left behind as she flew east over the roads we had just driven carved deep into my heart.

Renowned screenwriter Robert McKee says,

> A lifetime of story ritual has taught the audience to anticipate that the forces of antagonism provoked at the Inciting Incident will build to the limit of human experience, and that the telling cannot end until the protagonist is in some sense face to face with these forces at their most powerful.[4]

Coming face-to-face with my problems and my pain both excited and terrified me. I desperately wanted to escape this cave. I wanted freedom from the ache that plagued me. From the addiction I couldn't shake. From this life-numbing slumber.

I needed a new way. And I needed new people and new ideas and new graces to help me imagine it. It was now or never.

I had spent my whole life avoiding my story only to have it uproot everything. And now it was time. I breathed deeply and tried to keep that dot of light in view. As I considered McKee's words, I was overcome by the truth that I was just a man, living a real life. Not a hero in a movie. What would happen when I came "face to face with these forces at their most powerful"?

With no other good choices, I decided to find out.

PART TWO

Where
Have You
Come From?

9

The Liar

When I arrived in Seattle in August, I was twenty-six. In late summer the Pacific Northwest was in full force. The sun streamed through the mountains in the morning, bouncing off Lake Washington, then set gloriously over Puget Sound in the evening and dyed the ocean the color of fresh-squeezed orange juice. Between the bookends of the day, everywhere I looked I saw a miracle. Parks, paths, water. Bustling markets filled with craft food and drink.

What I came to realize, though, is that this beauty doesn't last. Come September, I knew I'd been entirely had. Seattle was a liar. The rain and wind and fog rolled in and basically never stopped. And if that wasn't enough, later that year the city experienced one of its very worst snowstorms ever. Being duped was a lesson I'd hoped to stop learning soon.

I lived in a four-bedroom house with six roommates. I showed up last, so I was given the smallest room, which was more of a closet with a closet. A couple of the guys attended the seminary with me, and the others were various mixtures of Southern transplants sowing their wild oats in the Pacific Northwest. Most worked as waitstaff, and one was a bartender slash writer who was composing the next great American novel exclusively by sending Hotmail emails back and forth to himself. It was a weird and rowdy crew. As social as I claimed to be, in undergrad I'd been a bit of a loner. As my addiction grew, so did my excuses for being alone or off somewhere else. But here there was a certain brotherhood I couldn't quite avoid. I'd also come to the end of things, so maybe I was just tired of fighting the possibility of community and intimacy. It probably helped that I was sometimes funny and a decent Player 2 at FIFA 2005 on Xbox.

Not only was Seattle a liar, but so was the seminary.

Since its inception, it had been operating out of a business park north of the city as the school sought funds to finish its new space downtown. It was to be a gem of a building, a cultural landmark right in the heart of the city. However, I was deflated to learn upon arrival that we would not be attending our inaugural semester in that shining new jewel in Belltown, Seattle. Instead, we'd continue to commute to the sprawling suburb of Bothell. And so, for the time being, this progressive, cutting-edge, exciting pinnacle of theological thought and psychological practice was to continue to hold its classes with a stellar view between the nine-to-five ladies huddled against the rain at ten in the morning with their Virginia Slims on one side and the chain taco joint with the delicious queso on the other.

To get to campus each morning, I had to drive through Madison Valley and past the neighborhood Starbucks that Howard Schultz frequented, which would soon become my new study hall. I'd head over Lake Washington on the floating bridge that I always feared would snap and carry me out to sea. Then on through a sprawling pine forest and into the business park to a school that was supposed to inspire a new way of living. Sad concrete offices with tinted windows covered in dusty, brown blinds went on as far as the eye could see. Delivery trucks motoring through their routes and bouncing over speed bumps passed gaggles of khaki pants and cornflower blue oxfords. I saw lots and lots of "business" but very little "park."

This? This is what I left my life for? *This* is where the epic struggle to sober up and change my life was to take place?

For the first few weeks, I pulled into the vast parking lot only to sit in my idling car as classes inside got underway. Had I made a terrible mistake? If not for KEXP, the local NPR station, playing Jamie Cullum from my new car stereo calming my nerves, I might have made a run for it.

Seattle turned cold. It no longer just lied; now it mocked as well.

To make matters worse, the school's property in the center of this beige hub of boring wasn't big enough for the first-year-student lectures, so those had to be held at a large Korean Evangelical Church nearby. My experience of community church space was the warm and homey cafetorium of my parish back home, where boxes of donuts were displayed after Mass each Sunday, not a sterile, blue-carpeted, white-walled multiuse cavern.

Things were getting worse by the second.

But the weather, the business park, and the interminably full rooms in which our classes were held became irrelevant when he walked in.

For it was in that fluorescently lit cavern that the man I'd underlined to death in Chicago, the man whose fault it was that I was here at all, the man who would become my mentor—Dan Allender—told us a tale that would become the second most important framing story in my life.

Faith, Hope, and Love was the foundational class of my two-year program, and in the context of those three words—words I'd heard my entire life—I was whisked into the stories of three ancient characters and given two questions that would change everything. If the story of Plato's cave had taken me this far, a story about an enslaved Egyptian was about to catapult me into something new.

———————————

That day, Dan bounded into the room from the hallway and darted to the podium set in front of our conference chairs and corporate folding tables. He was a strange mixture of mad scientist and wise sage. Thin and bony, he reminded me more of Scar from *The Lion King* than the friendlier, fuller version I'd come to know from the headshot on the back cover of his books that I'd ripped off and discarded. He was wearing what appeared to be a full suit of black foam armor. He'd taken up motorcycle riding and wanted to protect himself. The irony of what he was wearing wasn't lost on those of us paying attention to the way he began class, which was always . . . well . . .

interesting. Dan was famous for starting classes with a bang. Provocative thought-starters like these were not uncommon:

"Today we're going to talk about evil and violence in the context of your parents."

"Here are some of the ways you've come to hate yourself."

"Let's begin with a bit about masturbation and glory."

But on that particular day, he opened with a statement that would alter the way I was trying to exit the cave and do something with my story I'd never thought possible: save me from it.

"Hello," he said. "I'll jump right in. When you use the past to create a life in the present that is not open to the kindness, tenderness, grace, and mercy of God, you have used the past to form the future based on a commitment to self-protection."

And with that, this sapient sage in protective gear introduced us to the story of Hagar, an enslaved woman from Egypt; her mistress, Sarah; a man they called Abraham; and two questions that changed my life.

10

Hagar

Dan opened the Bible. "From Genesis, chapter 16," he began.

As he read aloud, my imagination sprung to life, transforming the deserts and tents of the ancient Middle East into ivory castles with balconies and forests laid with carpets of grass, damp with evening dew. Disappearing deep into my imagined version of events, the images flashed.

Another sleepless night. Desperation hangs heavy in the air like the fog rolling over the stone walls, emptying itself into the court.

Sarah stands on the balcony, staring into the gray abyss. Could she have flung herself into the mist and guaranteed her disappearance, she might have attempted it. And then a tiny thought with cosmic consequence: *Does a woman who cannot bear children even exist?*

Abraham stares at Sarah from the bed. Her silhouette glows in the space between midnight and dawn.

Anger first. *Why can't she?*

Shame next. *Is it me?*

He is humiliated but not yet humbled.

Quietly, he hums to himself. *Father Abraham . . . ha!* His anger swells. Hide or blame, he only has two gears.

He stands, moving toward her. Tenderness rises, but it's too much to hold on to for long.

She senses his presence and turns just so, careful not to offer her face. She knows what he is about to say.

"I'll fix it," he whispers sternly.

And with that, he's gone.

According to Jewish tradition, in Egypt there was a princess, the daughter to Pharaoh. Strong and lovely, her name was Hagar. She'd witnessed Sarah and Abraham's arrival in the court. Soon after, trouble followed. One terrible and horrific event after the other. Hagar watched from her own balcony as her people suffered and screamed in fear and heartache. She witnessed loss and surveyed death.

One evening, her father beckoned her. Guilt, shame, and fear twisted his aging face. Turning his eyes away from his daughter, he gestured toward Sarah and Abraham. And with that she was disowned. Given away as a gift. An offering. A "looks like your god is better than my god now scram" kind of present.

What could she do? What say did she have? What right to refuse her father?

Better to be a slave in the house of Sarah than an unwanted princess in my own, she lamented to herself.

As days turned into months turned into years, she could sense the distance between the unhappy couple. By now it was more of a chasm than mere marital disconnect. And she knew that if she were called upon to help bridge the great divide, she would have no choice—for she was still a slave, forced into captivity, even if she was royal at heart.

Then one evening, the moment Hagar had been dreading finally arrived. Sarah moves toward her slave. Tenderness rises as she takes Hagar in. Hagar, sensing Sarah's presence, turns just so but does not offer her face. She knows what Sarah is about to say.

"My husband is on his way," she whispers sternly.

Scripture skims over these next crucial moments with little more than a page turn and the passage of time: "So after Abram had been living in Canaan ten years, Sarai his wife took her Egyptian slave Hagar and gave her to her husband to be his wife. He slept with Hagar, and she conceived" (Gen. 6:3–4). But the truth is deeper and darker than this stark narrative skip. It's wholly gut-wrenching to read that a woman was literally given to another's husband. Understanding the cultural context doesn't correct the wrong. No scholarly knowledge can undo this sexual violence. No exegesis can erase the raw fact that this is rape. A woman no longer in her own land, with no rights to speak of, is forced to lie with and then carry the child of her abuser. It's no wonder Hagar is filled with rage when the cruel experiment is found to have worked.

Wounded and angry that her rape resulted in pregnancy, Hagar focuses her fury and indignation on her captor. The supposed alien now sits at an apex, carrying the hopes and dreams of a family that would not have given her the time of day otherwise. Morning sickness and crushing despair underscore the harsh reality of her predicament. She is with child.

But this fact does not unwind the tension between the couple as designed. Instead, the animosity between them roils. Sarah is enraged at the madness of the morality play they are in, humiliated at how it's all playing out. And she's not afraid to take her own anger out on her servant. With a firm hand, Sarah cracks the headlines: "You have no home. You are my slave. You are a prisoner. And you will do as I say."

The door slams shut.

It's late. Hagar no longer has tears left to cry. The fog again pours into the court, as is its nightly custom. She and her mistress are cosmically linked as she, too, imagines what it would be like to disappear into the mist.

Hagar's name is rich with multiple meanings. As she stares into the distance, each interpretation echoes through her belittled body and spirit, reverberating from the evening's latest punishment.

"You have no home." *Her name means stranger.*

"You are my slave." *To be dragged off.*

"You are a prisoner." *Pressed into service.*

"And you will do as I say." *Forsaken.*

The slamming door leaves Hagar alone with one more honorific description lingering in the air. *Flight.*

Her blank stare turns to resolve. She whispers to herself. "My name." It's in her and it's been there all along. "My name . . . means flight!"

She bolts, charging into the courtyard. With fog up to her knees, she looks as if she's gliding through a parting cloud. The gray mass breaks before her, leaving behind a wake of mist. It's freezing, though her brow beads with sweat. She rushes to the thick wooden gate—the last barrier to freedom. Pulling it open, she stands in the threshold.

No longer will you be a stranger, dragged off, pressed into service. No longer will you be forsaken. Instead . . . you will fly.

She sprints through the gate and a smile nearly makes its way onto her lips. The fog gives way to a dark wood, lit only by the moon dappled by the clouds. Damp branches grab at her as she fights through the thicket. Thorns ensnare her cloak and scrape her legs. One snags her soft cheek, plucking crimson. But she feels nothing save her feet hitting the cold, wet ground.

Just. Keep. Moving.

Her heart pumps from the depths. Finally, she breaks into the open of a clearing. She collapses to the grassy earth and heaves a guttural cry. Tears, blood, sweat, and dew mix as she presses her face into the cursed ground. She screams, letting the roots of her ancestors know her pain. She is desperate to split the earth in two with her cries, but it does not yield.

Wrapping her arms around her womb, she aches in agony with the knowledge that even here, far from her former prison, she is still trapped. Chained to herself. To the life she doesn't have and to the life growing within. She yells again, this time lifting her tearstained face to the sky like a wolf howling at the horizon. She drops again. Her hands grip the ground. All is silent save her breath.

A gentle breeze blows, sending the scent of the fragrant night deep into her lungs. For all the hurt she's expelled, finally, she takes in something fresh. It's not hope, not quite yet, but it's clean and crisp and carries with it the aroma of nearby water.

Then she hears it. The burble of a river. Entranced, she slowly lifts herself to her feet and follows the sound. She kneels, dipping her bloodied arm into the stream. The coolness stings as she washes her wounds. She splashes her face. She sips. She stands.

Suddenly, the ground shakes violently underfoot. Concentric circles push out from the center of the brook. A gust of wind nearly knocks her off her feet. Then, as quickly as the phenomenon began, the wind retreats, the water calms, and the shaking stops. She shivers. The hair on her dark bronze skin stands at attention as a voice calls out.

"Hagar."

The sound of her name being called pierces the night.

"Hagar."

She turns to face the path of her escape.

"Hagar."

The young woman turns back around and is greeted by a glowing warmth and love radiating from across the pool. A voice, enshrined by a glowing array—an angel of the Lord, speaking to her, asking her two questions that would change absolutely everything. "Where have you come from? Where are you going?"

The furious typing of fifty or so graduate students attempting to capture Dan's words verbatim snapped me back to attention. Leaning over the podium, he whispered the questions again.

"Where have you come from? Where are you going?"

Collapsed on my own kind of riverbank, I breathed those questions in like fresh air and could feel them become a part of me on a cellular level. Like Plato's cave story a decade earlier, this story of the enslaved Egyptian woman had undone me.

Later that semester, Dan would return to Hagar and tell us the rest of her tale, but for now we were left with an epic cliff-hanger.

As I gathered my things and moved outside, hungover from the haze I'd been floating in, I was greeted by a cold breeze that situated me next to Hagar at the water's edge. Side by side we stood, like two friends who knew each other's stories without saying a word. After all, we'd both just run away. Unblinking, I watched as she tilted her head just so, like a child listening to a parent describe the meaning of life. I followed her gaze, desperate to hear what she heard. I glanced at her hand and wanted to hold it, but didn't dare. Though kindred spirits, we didn't really know each other.

I'd stepped out from my daydream and into the parking lot of the Korean church as a third question floated into view. It wasn't one that Dan or the angel of the Lord had asked but rather one that had been building beneath the surface my entire life.

What do you do when someone asks you a question you know the answer to but cannot yet speak the truth?

I drove back through the jagged green pines, across the death-defying floating bridge, and took a left onto my new street. I parked as the Seattle spittle turned to sleet. As I headed up the creaky stairs to the porch filled with empty beer cans and overflowing ashtrays, the sleet morphed into snow, cooling my blood and soothing my mind. In a world that had turned upside down, the snow was familiar.

Family legend has it that I was born in the middle of a blizzard. As my mom gave birth, the nurses took bets on the exact time of my arrival while my grandmother anxiously scrubbed the floor of her kitchen with a toothbrush. Meanwhile, my dad sat drinking at the bar next to the hospital as the whole city experienced a whiteout.

I sat on the sagging couch my roommates had snatched from a corner on trash day, and like the snow, the angel's questions descended once more.

Where is it that I've come from?

Where is it that I'm going?

11

Called Out

The snow continued as I settled into my tiny closet with a closet and got to work on the small desk I'd managed to jam into the corner, thanks to an IKEA hack. The triangle of my existence that semester was limited to my room, school, and the local Starbucks. As I ferried myself between this triptych of locales, assignments rolled in. Syllabi. Reading requirements. And papers. So many papers. I'd sort of forgotten that seminary was also graduate school.

Almost everything we were asked to write involved using topics or themes from class to dive deeper into our personal stories. Assignments were designed to have us looking back through the chapters of our lives, seeking themes broad and small—excavating. A main tenet of the school held that if we wanted to understand how we got to where we were, we would need to understand from whence we came. The questions asked of Hagar were to be answered by us in written form. And so, in paper after paper inquiring about various aspects of my family of origin, I stated my story in the following predictable cadence, performed in a perfect three-act structure.

——— *Act 1* ———

I grew up in a diverse, sexually charged, blue-collar neighborhood. My dad was an alcoholic and sex addict who wasn't always around.

——— *Act 2* ———

My mom was a hardworking, single mom as well as a brittle diabetic prone to seizures. My brother and I took turns caring for her, force-feeding her orange juice whenever she seized.

——— *Act 3* ———

I was sexually abused by two older boys when I was ten.

——— *The End* ———

For months, I wrote various versions of those three acts and turned them in to my professors. In each iteration, I expanded on the details a bit more. I concluded early on, however, that I already had a pretty good idea of where I'd come from. No need to dig deeper, thank you very much. Besides, I had been confidently and readily telling these stories for years. I had no problem rattling off these startling details because they were dramatic. And interesting. They elicited attention, even sympathy—which I often used to great effect.

Along with this confidence came some solid storytelling skills. I knew exactly when to add a joke for laughs or when to punch up a line with a terribly sad phrase for a gut-wrenching closer. The tricks I'd learned onstage came in handy when telling the story of my life.

While writing these papers, I also took classes on Hebrew, human sexuality, and first-century history—standard fare for a school of theology and psychology. What I was not prepared for, though, was practicum groups. This part of the program was designed to reveal, with blistering honesty, the blind spots you carry as you relate to others, your story, and yourself.

Like the word *practicum* suggests, it was a place to practice. A place to practice bringing your whole self, a place to practice being human, a place to practice telling the truth. My soon-to-be best friend, Jarrod, also a first-year student, explained the work of practicum groups like this: "Practicum is the forced sharing of and listening to each other's stories so that we can find the deeper truths in all of our stories. The ultimate purpose is to see how we're all a part of one big story as we learn how we share similar pains, hopes, and desires."

Practicum groups were required and were facilitated by teacher's aides on track to become therapists, pastors, or professors. I'd sat in truth-telling circles like this before and figured it would be smooth sailing.

Because I'd entered school without any desire or intent to become a therapist or a pastor (you already know my feelings on becoming a priest), and because I thought I'd already "done the work," as they say, I just kept showing up each week with a catchy new spin on my well-told story. No need to practice if you already know how to play the game. Three acts, some jokes, and a single tear down the cheek. Next!

Until, one day, while I was putting the final flourish on my trio of pain, having plated it just so, I was rudely interrupted. Someone in my group blurted out, "I don't believe you."

I'd heard this phrase before. Remember Trudie? The take-no-crap acting teacher from Butler? The one whose number pirate-toothed Margaret needed? Well, "I don't believe you!" was her infamous catchphrase. When it was your turn to perform a scene or monologue and it became apparent that you weren't connected to the moment, hadn't inhabited the character, or were simply phoning it in, she'd call out from the darkness of the black box theater:

"I don't believe you!"

Trudie wasn't being cruel, she just wanted to be clear. "What good is telling a story if you aren't going to tell the truth?" she would yell. In theater school I gladly took such drill sergeant—type direction. I wanted to be good at getting into the skin of a character and understanding their story so well that I could honorably tell it. Here, however, the story I was attempting to peddle was not made up. It was my own. The callout felt preposterous while I was sitting in a circle with a bunch of therapist slash pastor wannabes. I was indignant.

"What do you mean, you don't believe me?" I shot back.

"This is the third time you've told us this story. I'm not saying it's not true. I'm not saying it didn't happen in the way that you're saying that it did. But you just seem . . . so . . . completely disconnected from it. It seems like you're just—"

"Telling you my story," I interrupted. "That's what we're supposed to be doing here, right?"

"But you're not telling us your story."

"Then what is it that *I am* doing?" My voice felt tight against the back of my throat.

My sparring partner held the room for a beat. And then, with precision, said, "You're performing it."

"Performing it!?"

There was a painful silence. My eyes darted around the circle, inviting someone, anyone, to give me a look that joined in my outrage. No takers. My classmates knew I didn't need to be rescued from this truth. I needed to hear it. With a kind of gentle firmness, she continued.

"And if you'd have the courage ..."

"*Courage?!*" I growled.

"It's brave to tell us the facts of these stories. But you're stuck retelling the facts—"

"Oh, come on! You're not even a real therapist, you're just ..." I trailed off like a child forgetting the rest of his insult.

"If you had the courage to ... dig a little deeper. To inch a little closer ... maybe something in you could shift. Maybe these stories could change you. Move you. Instead of you using them to try to move us."

My face was hot with shame. Caught, but nowhere near willing to admit it, I sputtered, "Great, thanks for that."

The tension in that small room suspended us all. No one moved a muscle. It was quiet except for the hum of the half-dozen white noise machines on the other side of the door that lined the long hallway of practicum rooms.

I fantasized about picking up my chair and throwing it through the wall, hulk-smashing the white noise into nothing, forever annihilating whatever other idiotic story sessions were happening throughout the hall.

Instead, I looked at the clock. Three minutes of my time remained. My eyes felt swollen and red with held-back tears as I leveled my gaze at my foe. With fury roiling in my gut, I silently counted down all 180 seconds.

The next morning, still seething from the sting of being confronted, I entered the Korean church a few minutes late and found a spot in the back row. I wasn't interested in seeing my practicum group. Nor was I interested in being seen by them.

I pulled out my laptop and opened it quietly, so as not to disturb the teacher's aide giving the class announcements. But when my finger nicked the power button it "bonged" loudly to life. My seething turned to shame as the class turned to locate the interruption. My eyes caught those of my peers who hadn't saved me from myself the day prior. I felt small and helpless, like a kid whose only option is a tantrum. But before I could embarrass myself further by blurting out the spiteful comment starting to bubble up behind my lips, Dan took the podium and launched in.

"Faith, hope, and love are the nature of what it means to be made in the image of God. They are the very essence of *what* we are to become and *how* we are meant to get there. And how we get there is through the particularities of our stories."

This guy. Always with the stories.

He continued, "So, let's take it from the top, shall we? One word at a time. *Faith*. Faith is a remembrance of the goodness of your rescue, of redemption. It is when goodness has come, not because of your own effort, your own design, or your own accomplishment, but because a gift has been bestowed that has altered the trajectory of the story you're engaged in. In other words, the nature of faith is an intrusive moment of goodness that you cannot will, you cannot plan, and you cannot control. Put even more simply, faith comes by remembrance. You must remember your stories. You must remember the particular moments.

"So rather than looking at your story from ten thousand feet, what would it mean for you to move down to five thousand feet? And if at five thousand, what would it mean for you to move to five hundred feet? And if five hundred, why not five?"

I was typing furiously, trying to keep up, when he said something that collided each of my worlds into a massive explosion of meaning.

"Plato apparently said that every story has a beginning, a middle, and an end. That's a lovely way of putting it. But I would venture to say that your story is much more nuanced. Because while the beginning of your story has innocence, it has also tragedy. And as you dig into the stories of your life, hunting for these moments of faith, you will find yourself in the midst of a troubling paradox. Because it will be in the deepest and darkest places, the locales of trouble itself, the rooms coupled with the most innocence and the most tragedy, where the radical change will occur."

I stopped typing. Perhaps the group had been right. I caught the reflection of my weary face in my computer screen. I wanted radical change to occur. I needed it. It's why I was here. Resigned, yet again, I allowed myself a quiet thought: *Maybe I can try looking closer.*

Dan warned that it wouldn't be easy. In fact, he said remembering would be like going into battle. Because engaging in a story war would mean entering into heartache.

"And at the center of it all," he declared, "you will have to wrestle with the most fundamental question of all: 'Is God good?'"

Whatever calm curiosity I felt smashed to smithereens at the audacity of this question. I'd heard this one before. The one that goes, "Even though that horrible thing happened to you, God is still good."

I shot my hand in the air almost reflexively. Dan nodded, and I cleared my throat.

"I guess that's where I'm getting tripped up. How, in all these terrible stories you're asking us to remember, is there any kind of goodness at all?"

"Good question. I'll say this: If there is a God or anything like God at all, then God is present—in the suffering and the joy. But God's presence doesn't take away suffering, it intensifies it. This presence then invites us into engagement with His heart. Our suffering opens doors to understanding the suffering of God. His suffering allows us to enter and understand our own."

I bristled. "But how? That's insane. Why would a 'good God' need us to understand *His* suffering? Why not just take it away in the first place? I can't believe in a God that's like that!"

"Amen," he calmly responded.

Amen?!

But before I could say another word, he launched back in.

"Do you hear what he's saying, class? If faith is remembering, it can't be without doubt. Maybe the highest mark of what it means to be a Christian is your willingness to blaspheme. To doubt. To question so deeply that God is present in your suffering, or didn't prevent the harm, or that He's good, or even that He exists at all. Listen. Whatever this life is, whatever this thing we call the gospel is, we must say it is a call to wholeness, to reconciliation. And if it is about making peace, we must have the courage to enter the divide. Without the capacity to enter into the war of your own story, into the depths of your own abyss and addictions, and despair, and pain and trauma, then whatever faith you eventually come to will only mute your troubled heart as you attempt to domesticate a truly wild God."

Leaning over the podium once more, he drove it home. "Here is the truth: the more that you enter the particulars of your story, the more grief you'll find and the more you'll see that your story is a gloriously whole mix of innocence and tragedy, of death and resurrection—frankly, of faith: the remembrance of goodness in the midst of the most unholy grit. If faith is remembrance, what do you remember? Or in other words, Blaine, tell me: Where have you come from?"

12

Caught

And the book says: we may be through with the past, but
the past ain't through with us.

Jimmy Gator, from the movie Magnolia

I sulked myself back from class that afternoon, landing in a
corner of Starbucks. Alone at a tiny table with my computer,
over a steaming cup of bitter coffee, I nursed the notion of
going deeper. As the blinking cursor of an untitled document
steadily pulsed with provocation, I opened myself up to my
tale one more time. I sunk deeper into the stories I thought
I'd already told. Wanting to truly know where I'd come from,
I hunted for this thing called faith. And then I began to type.

What do *I remember?*

The heat is hot on my nine-year-old face. I should be looking
at the floaty white stuff, but the yellow ball beckons instead. I

wrap my hands together, shaping them into a tube, and press them to one eye, closing the other. Squeezing lightly, I can control how much light gets in. From glowing, burning brightness to total darkness. A tighter grip ushers me into an inky black abyss and I panic. But when I open my little hands just so, I breathe again as relief comes into view: the light at the end of the tunnel.

"That one looks like a big car," she says.

I remove my hands, letting them flop on the scratchy green grass, and squint. I rub my face, my eyes readjusting to focus on the cloud she's pointing at.

"More like your dad's semitruck, maybe," I reply.

We lay on my front lawn. The grass is still damp even though it's well past noon. August in Minnesota is humid, and everything always feels heavy and wet no matter the time of day.

She turns her head toward me. "So . . . you want to?"

We move from the sun and hide ourselves in the shade under the deck of my split-level duplex. The hunky air conditioner, dented from the hits it's taken from errant soccer balls, squats next to us and blows the hottest of air into our faces. We stand facing each other in this muggy cocoon, accompanied only by the heated wind that makes it hard to breathe. In that moment I realize how my pet bunny, Floppy, died the summer before. I'd foolishly thought putting her cage next to the air conditioner outside would keep her cool. It was a shaded place, next to an appliance whose job was to keep things cold. What I'd not known is that it only kept the *inside* chilly while jacking up the temperature outside. I'd found Floppy with her tiny rabbit teeth wrapped around one of the metal bars. She'd died trying to escape.

So, there we were: me, the girl, the air conditioner, and the empty cage in which I'd accidentally killed last year's family Easter present.

"On the count of three," she whispered.

I nodded.

"One. Two. Three."

And with that we pulled our respective pants down around our ankles.

My heart thumped. Sweat trickled down my arm. Our eyes bounced about, neither of us sure where to look. Eye contact felt impossible, but because the basement window reflected our naked bits, we could sneak glances without having to look . . . well . . . right at them.

And then, without warning, just behind our prepubescent reflections, an angry face came into view.

The genius of a split-level home is that you can have a basement without the cost of digging all the way underground. The result is this half-basement situation where the windows sit at ground level. So . . . say you're standing under your deck with your pants around your ankles, and your dad happens to come downstairs to watch a college football game. Because of the cleverly placed windows, he will most certainly have a front-row seat to the other show taking place outside.

My eyes darted from my dad's to hers, but she was already on the run. I looked back to the window to find my dad gone too. I limped out from under the deck and attempted to make a run for it. I watched as she made it past the border between our backyards and to apparent safety. I ran in the same direction, or tried to anyway, but I tripped over myself and tumbled with my feet twisted up in my underwear.

As I desperately hopped along, I saw my dad's shadow approaching from behind. The sun I'd been staring at earlier had dropped closer to the horizon and elongated his dark shape until I was engulfed by it. One more awkward hop and I was caught. His fingernails dug into my armpits as he swooped me up and spun me back toward the house.

He marched me inside and up the stairs, bellowing out to my mom. Tears slid down my sweaty face, and my cheeks flushed with shame.

"Kino!" my dad screamed my mom's college nickname.

Then he dangled me before her shocked face, roaring.

"Do you know what your son has been doing?"

Back in the Starbucks, I stopped typing. I couldn't peck out another word. The afternoon sun had turned to rain as I packed up my things and walked home. Over the next few days, whether in the coffee shop or in my tiny room, I combed through the details of this story. Later that week I shared it with my practicum group. The new details brought new questions.

What did I find in my father's face?

What did I learn about myself that day? And was it true?

What was I left to think about my own little body? About curiosity? About the dynamic between my parents?

Where had this story, as it collided with my dad's story, gotten embedded?

*What did I learn about getting caught? About what to do
when you catch someone else?*

*How did this story become a setup for my abuse the following
year and my own addiction in the years to follow?*

As I underwent this terrifyingly honest process, I was startled by a realization. I began to understand it was not, as I had always believed, the event *itself* that lodged a shameful story in my past. It was what happened *after*. It was my interpretation and the meaning I assigned to the event. I realized it was the reaction from my dad and the lack of care that followed that gave this story its real and lingering power.

Listening to my classmates respond to this story with kindness, tenderness, and grief for that nine-year-old boy under the deck forced me to look at it again. And as I contemplated the rage and disgust I'd seen on my father's face, I understood I'd been invited to look at myself with the exact same fury and contempt. In a sense, this was much more a story about my father than it was about me. His reaction gave him away. In that one moment, I was invited to turn on my young self. To curse my curiosity. And most important of all, to learn to hide better, because getting caught meant humiliation.

As my practicum group helped me name this horrible lie, I began to grieve the reality that nobody had helped me see there might be safer or more appropriate spaces and places to bring my normal questions and curiosity. It wasn't my shame that had left me all alone. I'd been handed a bucketful of my father's wounds and then been cast aside. He'd hoisted up a mirror to his own mortification and called it mine. Mistaking my face for his, I took that mirror from his hands and held on tight.

Together, in that tiny practicum room, sometimes gently and sometimes with ferocity, we fought for the truth. As the months ticked by, I started to shift my relationship with that old, embedded story. My relationship to its meaning and my relationship to myself. And sure enough, a miracle unfolded. I began to do the impossible: I began to change the past.

As I dug deeper, it seemed that it wasn't in the event itself that I was to locate the elusive thing Dan called "faith." Rather, I began to see it in the razor-thin space between the event and what happened right after. And as I pried open the crack between those two moments, I found goodness and grace and, somehow, peace. Maybe even God.

Perhaps there were good gifts to uncover in this messy, painful, sacred, intentional practice of remembering after all.

13

Telling on Myself

I now knew that hidden away in my stories were important truths I desperately needed to unearth if I wanted them to stop dictating my life. So I hunted for the particularities. I kept digging. What was hiding in plain sight that might help me understand where I'd come from?

Recovery had afforded me some practice. It taught me that the best place to start was to tell on myself. I tried to zero in on the stories with details that would prefer to stay hidden. The only problem was that sometimes telling on myself meant telling on other people too.

Naming the truth about my parents felt like betrayal. They had done the best they could with what tools they had. Unfortunately, their lack of tools had consequences. I know my mom had her hands full as an often-single mom to two boys. Faced with the difficult task of supporting my brother and me in that unknown, uneasy space spouses try to hold with their addicted partners, codependence became an addiction of its own.

As their marriage continued to play out in broken circles, my mom grabbed on to me in unhealthy ways, silently asking me to husband her. How could she not? She carried so much trauma lingering from her own childhood: being fathered by a violent yet charming alcoholic while managing her own chronic illness. Her style of relating to my dad, and subsequently to me, only yielded more brokenness and left me unprotected in some essential ways. Although I had often casually rattled off the details of these facts, I knew there was a story hidden in the weeds that needed some attention.

With pen and paper this time, I carefully etched the question that had, by now, become a mantra: *What do you remember?*

On a clear afternoon, I ran up our wide cement steps and onto the creaky porch we'd just stained another tone of brown. The chemical scent of the stain mingled with the aroma of the lilac bush blooming to the left of the front door and hung in the air as I passed the threshold and went into the air-conditioned house. It was silent, but I already knew what sound would come next. Always at the ready, I'd developed a sixth sense related to my mom. The reverberations of her convulsions would sometimes wake me at night almost before they happened. She'd turned to me as a savior and husband-like figure when it became clear that my dad would be unable to hold that station. Only seven, I'd already been trained to be an expert when it came to her care.

I stepped onto the first stair just as the sound of her skin slapping the linoleum met my ears. I sprinted up into the kitchen to find her seizing on the floor. This was not a new sight to my young eyes, but I was still shocked. Her brittle, thin, runner's body convulsed. My heart raced and my hands shook as I jumped into action. I pulled a plastic cup from the cupboard and filled it with the magical elixir known as orange juice from frozen concentrate. I knelt down and pulled her sweaty head into my lap, parted her lips, and pressed the cup against her clenched teeth, hoping some of the juice would make its way past this armored entrance and into her bloodstream. The cup shook, splashing the sticky orange stuff all over the place. The veins in her temples swelled. I'd never been more scared in my life. This time felt more serious. What had worked so often in the past wasn't working now. Unsure what else to do, my terrified seven-year-old self ran. I barged out the door and back into the heat, screaming for help throughout the neighborhood. I banged on doors. Begged someone to call an ambulance.

Paramedics shortly arrived and were able to regulate my mom's blood sugar levels. As she lay on the stretcher, recovering from the intense pressure to her brain, she turned toward me and, without blinking, said, "You could have just given me more orange juice."

I didn't know what to say. Any relief I'd felt that help had arrived and the crisis had been averted vanished. I was still in shock, adrenaline still coursing through my system. But now I was also confused. And, worse, embarrassed. *But what should I have done?* It wasn't that I longed for her to thank me. I longed to not be responsible for these kinds of decisions. I wanted someone to check on me. To tell me that it was OK to ask for help.

The message from my mother was loud and clear: the cavalry was not coming. And while I longed to be cared for, to feel safe and protected, it would be me looking out for her. And even then, I might be reprimanded.

It was not my mom's fault she had a chronic illness. We all wished she'd had the fortune of better health. Still, I found myself frustrated that I had to pretend this volatility didn't affect me and that it didn't keep me on high alert. This all carried great grief, because while I didn't want to resent my mother, being forced to regularly take on this adult role, without honest conversations, put me strangely in the middle of my parents' marriage, a place I did not want to be.

As I shared that story on paper and in practicum, I saw how it, and so many other nearly identical events, set me up to leave home the second I was able and not come back. My decision was more than just the gutsy move of an aspiring, hungry-to-succeed, driven artist. Sure, there was something I was moving toward. But there was also something I was trying to escape. This also set up the same ambivalent push and pull I would employ in my own intimate relationships. And it only reinforced the unpredictability and fear of waiting for the other shoe to drop.

In my heartache over this specific catalog of stories, I still attempted to locate compassion. My parents were unwittingly passing down and re-creating pieces of their own untended-to stories. While I knew many of the traumatic and abusive stories of their pasts, I'd never know them all. It's no surprise, really, that they'd found each other. I recognized that they didn't exist simply as my parents but they, too, came from somewhere. They, too, wrestled with their own demons. The fact remained that I loved my parents, and I held this love in tension with the ways in which their traumatic pasts, individually and shared, informed what would become my traumatic past.

Seattle was taking names—mine particularly. I came for healing, but things were getting harder. I knew I was getting closer to stories I really needed to tell. By this time, I'd panic-sweated, cried, and slammed my computer closed in rage in coffee shops all over the city. The problem now was that I'd come too far to turn back around. I'd begun to name the shadows within my cave. I'd passed beyond the fire and was now scrambling through the dark tunnel, hunting for that dot of light. Forced to rely on emerging skills and brand-new senses to make my way through, I was worn out. Would it ever get easier? Was there really more? More than the next high, the next hit? Was there something more creative, more whole, more human? Something invisible urged me forward.

And it wasn't all terrible. I was making new friends. Real friends, who held my stories and still wanted to play FIFA and Wii Tennis with me. I was laughing. I was coming up for air and then diving back into the reading and writing.

I kept digging deeper, trying to answer—really answer—the question, *Where have you come from?* The stories I'd only been performing kept asking to be re-penned and mined for their particulars. If I was going to hold hope for where I was going, I needed to keep talking about where I'd been.

14

Possibility

The summer before my abuse, I saw a flyer taped to the glass door at Tom Thumb, our local convenience store, advertising tryouts for the musical *The Wizard of Oz* at the Blaine High School Community Theater. It was a sign in all the ways a sign can be a sign. A totem. An omen. A prophecy. I plucked the parchment from the door, pedaled home on my red Schwinn I'd taught myself to ride, and begged my mom to take me to the audition.

Performing has a long history in my family, from vaudeville to some of Minnesota's most prestigious farm-town playhouses. Relatives have gone to try to make it in LA, started theater companies, and played in rock bands. This would not be my first time in a theater, but it was my first audition.

Every theater has the same smell. The cavernous space between the stage and the seats holds the pungent aromas of sawdust and makeup. The scent of stale popcorn and the burnt edges of plastic gels, fuses, light bulbs, and make believe waft about. The room, whether empty or full, is electrically charged with the greatest of all the things: possibility.

When the day came, my mom signed me in and we headed to a pair of open seats near the aisle. My small frame was engulfed by the hinged seat. Sweat beads formed behind my knees. The seat fabric scratched against my bare legs. Everyone looked a little dressed up, and I wished I'd worn pants instead of shorts. For the next hour or so, grownups and kids took the stage one at a time. They told jokes and serious stories with funny accents. One guy shouted a monologue from *Beverly Hills Cop 3*, but most people sang a song accompanied by a pianist onstage. I was enthralled and could feel something happening in my body. I settled in. I breathed. I smiled. My knee sweat began to dry up. I felt so at home.

"Blaine Hogan!"

The man who shouted my name wore a chunky, oatmeal-colored sweater draped around his shoulders. He held a pair of wire-rimmed glasses attached to thin rope up to his face and peered through them at his clipboard.

"*Blaine* Hogan?"

As he said my name again, I detected an elevated, unfamiliar accent. Like he grew up in Brainerd, went to U of M in the city for undergrad, watched a lot of PBS, and perhaps had grander visions for himself than directing community theater.

He must be the director, I thought, as I scurried to the front of the auditorium.

"Yep. Here."

"Interesting name. Go on, then."

I headed up the stairs, moved to the center, and made my way to the edge of the stage. The warm lights pulled everything out of focus. I squinted and I smiled—and I was silent.

"And what do you have for us, Blaine from Blaine?" his voice called out from the dark.

"Huh?"

The lady at the piano piped up.

"What song have you prepared, sweetie?"

Fresh sweat formed behind my knees, threatening to drown me in my own shoes. The liquid was blocked only by the tiny frozen hairs standing at attention.

I had not prepared a song. But I was quick on my feet.

"I know what *that* kid sang." I pointed into the theater.

And with that, the pianist counted me in. "And-a one, two, three, four!"

For my efforts, I was awarded the role of Lollipop Guild Number Two and my world debut into theater. A place that would become a safe haven, until it was one no longer.

I could not help but bless my young courage. I'd found a place to feel alive. I'd walked myself, excited but unsure, up the stairs and onto a stage in front of strangers who were literally there to evaluate me and determine if I was good enough. Some people crumble in those moments. But the thrill of being seen made me soar. All my senses were totally heightened. I had not only made it through the experience but had been found good enough. What a relief. I would be allowed to return for weeks of rehearsals, to pretend and play and create something out of nothing. This was my introduction to the magic of making art from an imaginary place.

True to form, from that day on I dove in deep. I'd circle auditions in the classifieds every Sunday and beg my mom to take me. Modeling and acting classes in downtown Minneapolis became routine. And whether it was a community or children's theater production, a school play, or just asking my fourth grade teacher if I might put up a brief scene from a volume of the Hardy Boys series by way of dramatic monologue instead of writing a book review, I fell in love with the idea that through this medium I could literally become someone else.

I also found that theater people were my people. We were the outcasts and the weirdos. And no matter who I was, who I wanted to be, or who my family was, the theater was a place where I could belong. Oh, and the attention was lovely. And something I genuinely longed for.

The theater also provided entry into colleges, scholarships, and real, live, actual paying acting gigs that took me around the country. When I graduated from college with a degree in theater performance, I packed up and set off to become a professional actor. The work took me to some crazy places and even crazier gigs, starting with my very first paying job at the Astor's Beechwood Mansion living history museum, where on odd-numbered days I was an aristocrat from 1891, giving tours with my fellow cast members. On even-numbered days I acted as a servant character from the United Kingdom. It was all manner of hullabaloo, as the managers housed this group of ten actors in their twenties in the servants' quarters on the third floor of the mansion. When there wasn't a private function or ball or wedding going on, we'd have the whole place to ourselves. We'd make grilled cheese in the fancy kitchen or hold dance parties in the grand ballroom. While I made only $90 a week, it was a great beginning to the life of a traveling actor.

When I was between gigs, I did corporate promotions such as dressing up as a referee and assaulting morning commuters with free boxes of Smart Start cereal. I'd blast a Kellogg's branded whistle I'd been supplied and yell at women in their fifties just trying to make it to work on time: "Time out, lady! Looks like you could use a Smart Start to your day!" Then I'd toss a box her way. Many fell to the sidewalk. Some came whizzing back in my direction.

I was also the Tutti-Frutti man, the Pepto Bismol man, and I once wore a Cellbie the Cellphone blow-up suit in which I was routinely tackled and kicked by teenagers.

While it seemed I'd take any work, I did appear to have some boundaries. On one occasion I turned down the national tour of *Sesame Street Live*. I'd auditioned to be one of the non-costumed kids who sang and danced their way through the show, and when they called, I was elated.

"So, we know you wanted a non-costume role, but we do have something else open immediately that would get you on the tour and a better chance of a different part in the future," the lady on the other end of the line teased.

Bert? Ernie? Big Bird? Oscar? I wondered.

"The role is for the back half of Mr. Snuffleupagus."

My work ran the gamut from a one-man show where I played a transexual German rockstar named Hedwig, which sold out extended performances, to an incredibly mediocre four-month run of *Guys and Dolls* in Coral Springs, Florida, to being on a television show, to being flown to New York City and put up in a hotel to audition for the producers of a new Broadway musical. I hustled for gig after gig after gig. While each opportunity advanced my career, each role also offered me the chance to become someone else. To disappear from my real life into the backstory and drama of someone else's. And as nerve-wracking as performing could be, it was far easier than being myself.

But as my career grew, so did my ambivalence. Being an actor is simultaneously one of the most communal professions and one of the loneliest. If you're lucky enough to work, you find yourself held by the most loving and generous feeling one moment and utterly alone the next. Because when the applause finally dies, you're left to silently retreat to your hotel or apartment on your own.

As I sank into this loneliness, I sunk deeper into the wounds I'd endured as a kid. Online porn turned into random meetups into dalliances I spent my meager earnings on. I used and used and used. I lied and lied and lied. Two traits addicts are famous for.

As I told these stories in Seattle, I began to learn an uncomfortable yet holy truth: the things that protected you as a child, that allowed you to survive, often become the things that eventually try to destroy you as an adult. Over time, the theater, the gig-jumping, and the travel simply offered more and more opportunities for me to hide. I was a terrible jerk to a lot of people I loved and an even bigger jerk to the ones who loved me. As a result, I lost friendships and relationships and began to lose my grip on myself. Even the professional success I had mustered wasn't enough to save me.

When I thought of that first panic attack back in Chicago, the thing that finally broke it all wide open, the biggest alarm my body could sound, I felt gratitude.

This is the gift of hitting rock bottom. Of coming to the end of yourself. You smash to the ground. Everything finally breaks. A bajillion little pieces explode into the atmosphere. You feel like dying. But somewhere, just on the other side of it all coming apart, there is also relief in naming things for what they are. This is where the work of rebuilding can finally begin, and this was the work I'd come to do.

15

No One to Tell

My neighborhood contained a cornucopia of sexual experimentation and exposure. I saw, experienced, and heard things that were way beyond my years. And although I often had a sense in the pit of my stomach that something wasn't quite right, I had no language for it. Nobody was available, or even able, to help me process experiences I didn't understand. I often felt alone and unprepared. I was supposed to act like these things were OK and also understand I was not supposed to talk about them.

Stacks of *Playboy* magazines sat in garages and next to toilets in more than a few bathrooms. All sorts of versions of spin the bottle were played that moved quickly beyond seven minutes in heaven. In certain homes, porn casually played on TVs in the background, watched by parents as kids ran around in easy view. The adults never seemed embarrassed by their behavior, nor did they seem concerned about any effect it might have on the children.

And yet it wasn't until I started telling these stories that I realized the true impact of these environments. Of course, it affected the children. I know it affected me.

There were several stories I could have selected to remember from this bizarre neighborhood dynamic. But I knew it was time to tell the ones that had gotten the most stuck.

The summer after I'd entered Munchkin Land, it happened. I was ten.

M and S were the unofficial leaders of our little gang of latch-key kids and were maybe six or seven years older than the rest of us. M's dad drove big rigs for a living. I never met S's parents. M lived behind us and S's house was down the street and one block over. M was an expert at sneaking out undetected. S's parents had mirrors all over the house and owned a waterbed with a zebra-print cover.

I needed someone older to talk to. To tell things to. Someone to confide in. To ask questions. They'd both taken a liking to me, and I was desperate for the care.

Is your mom still sick?

I heard your dad last night. Rough, man. Believe me, I know.

Once again facing the blinking cursor, I tucked myself and my laptop into my twin bed in Seattle and attempted to recall the particularities of the tales I hadn't told.

One story at a time.

———— *M* ————

In the basement, my dad's scent hangs in the air. I stand at the vanity staring at the water dripping into the plastic cup, placed to mute the leaky faucet. The faded blue paint comes into view as my hands grip the fake marble sink. In the mirror, M's face appears behind me. "If you want to be good, you're going to have to practice," he says. *What does he mean?* I am confused but can't find my voice. His visage disappears and I'm left with only myself to look at. As it happens, I clutch the stone vanity, holding on for dear life. One second more and the counter might crumble between my tiny fingers.

———— *S* ————

It's summer and joyous chaos is everywhere. With very few fences to slow us down, we sprint the length of the block without stopping, cutting through the heart of the neighborhood and everyone's backyard. We dodge dogs and hurdle swing sets. Somehow, we break away from the pack and end up in his driveway. S invites me in and takes me up to his parents' room. It's cool and quiet. A magazine is spread out on the zebra-print bed. The fleshy photos glisten as the pages bob, floating on the waterbed and catching the late afternoon sun. The door shuts behind him and he moves toward me. I crash into the sea and feel like I'm being trampled by a stampede of black and white hooves.

There is nobody to tell.

I don't even know what *to* tell. I am embarrassed and afraid. Everything is all mixed up. My little life moves in slow motion.

I feel both terror and excitement. It is like being told a secret I don't want to know.

And then, like being catapulted out of a cannon, everything picks up speed as I spend the next two decades trying to recapture the feeling from these two moments. I crave the warm safety of the high, of the attention. I even find myself wanting the shame that immediately follows. I realize that if I press the buttons on the cable box fast enough on that one channel after midnight, I can make out bodies between the fuzz of the screen. I padlock the box I've filled with magazines stolen from bathrooms and garages. I find my way onto phone sex lines and into online chat rooms.

Am I different now? Can everyone tell? Does everyone know? Or am I the only one? I fold into myself and work on memorizing the lyrics to "We Didn't Start the Fire" in my bedroom. And the most harmful of all the aftereffects, I hide.

After I'd written these stories, the familiar cadence of sharing them with my group followed. These were details I'd never uttered. And yet, telling secrets in the presence of safe faces was profound. Not only did my practicum group hold the details, the tears, and the anguish with me, but they also gave me the care and kindness I'd been missing for years. And the greatest gift wasn't just that they were kind to me but that, somewhere along the way, they helped me find kindness for myself. When a person is seen, really seen, and then loved, really loved, it does something powerful to their heart: it coaxes them out of hiding.

16

Hiding and Being Seen

Dan eventually returned us to the story of Hagar. The questions that disrupted her were doing a number on all of us. But there was another part of her story that captured me. Hagar's encounter with the angel was confusing and complicated. How do you account for such violence and apathy toward a woman? I certainly could not. And yet, it is there, hidden in the heart of her story, between the both/and, that we find something wholly remarkable: the first account in the Bible of a human naming God.

Laura Merzig Fabrycky described it beautifully in her essay "God Is Not Elsewhere."

> An Egyptian slave woman is the biblical character who makes this point so capably. An early poet of the faith, Hagar calls God *El Roi*, the God who sees me (Gen. 16:13), and God welcomes this creative and truthful honorific. This abandoned woman could see, in the midst of her own personal earthquakes

of rejection and brutal domestic violence, that God could see her, which gave her life and hope. This precious name of God reminds us that we too are seen by God if we have the eyes to see him where we are, *to see him seeing us*. We often need help with that. We need prophets and poets to point him out and to point out the possibilities.[1]

I knew something about personal earthquakes. But I struggled to consider that God saw me. And if He did, was that even something I wanted? Looking to the poets and prophets, and Bible stories I was assigned to read and exegete, I dove in to see what I could find. Their ancient words helped me begin to get my brain around the idea of being seen. But it was the unlikely prophets and poets in my own story who started to get to my heart. They stood in as proxies until I could see what Hagar so clearly saw.

El Roi, the God who sees me.

———————————

My friend Jarrod believes most of us hide because we either feel like God is judging us because we are bad or feel we are unworthy and won't risk the vulnerability because God is good. So, we hide. We turn away. We force distance. We create space.

This reveals more about the way many of us imagine God than it does about God's actual character. This hiding business isn't new to humanity. We've been doing it for a long time, in fact. Let's call it learned behavior.

Go all the way back to Genesis 3, for example. The story unfolds with the whirlwind of creation. Delight abounds and all is well. But it does not stay that way.

When the woman saw that the fruit of the tree was good for food and pleasing to the eye, and also desirable for gaining wisdom, she took some and ate it. She also gave some to her husband, who was with her, and he ate it. Then the eyes of both of them were opened, and they realized they were naked; so they sewed fig leaves together and made coverings for themselves.

Then the man and his wife heard the sound of the LORD God as he was walking in the garden in the cool of the day, and they hid from the LORD God among the trees of the garden. But the LORD God called to the man, "Where are you?"

He answered, "I heard you in the garden, and I was afraid because I was naked; so I hid." (vv. 6–10)

I was afraid, so I hid.

Oh, how predictably human.

I understood this impulse to hide. To feel so ashamed of something I'd done or so afraid of being caught that I'd rather disappear than allow the truth to be found out. In many ways, so much of my life followed that pattern. I hid until finally— thank God—my life fell apart. The lies couldn't hold up any longer, and the shame stopped being stronger than the possibilities to come if the truth were fully known.

Hiding is exhausting. Fig leaves aren't easily made into clothing, and eventually God comes walking through the garden in the cool of the day looking for us.

As an undergrad, I had an amazing history professor named Dr. Porter. It was his first year teaching at Butler. He was a nerd. And I loved him. He was incredible at making history interesting, which made this mandatory-for-theater-majors class almost pleasurable. Turns out, he was interested in theater as well, and so we'd often chat after class.

Now, I mostly didn't do what they called "homework" in college. I did the barest of bare minimums. Distracted by preparing for life as a professional actor, my unofficial motto was, "Cs and Ds get degrees!" When it came time to turn in our final papers for the semester, I didn't have one to turn in. Unwilling to face any consequences, I sought out a burgeoning new technology in 2001 called an "internet search engine." All night long I searched for work I could—how do you say?—*borrow* from.

I copied and pasted, and the next day I handed in my paper with a big smile on my face and walked right out the door. Three days later, as grades were starting to post, I got an email from Dr. Porter:

Blaine, your paper is under review for plagiarism. I'd like to speak with you.

I was caught. But maybe I could get out of it. Surely I'd bamboozled my way out of worse.

Shepherding me into his office, Dr. Porter seemed heavy. As he sat down across from me, his face looked more than disappointed; he was hurt. It wasn't often that I'd stuck around long enough in any mess I'd made to see the aftermath in real time. Because it was his first year, Dr. Porter explained, he needed to make an example of me. Also, I should be thankful the extent of my punishment was just failing his class. Apparently my plagiarism was so egregious he'd had to fight the department out of straight-up expelling me.

"So, I must ask. Did you write this paper?" His voice carried the burden of broken trust.

I had an enormous choice to make. I could sing the song my dad taught me. I could double down on the lie. I could deny, deny, deny. I could blame. I could cause a scene. I could run. I could hide. But I was tired of that old tune. With a pitiful sigh, I tried something new.

"No. I didn't write it."

It might have been the first time I'd really told the truth. I'm glad I did. Because I was not prepared for what he was about to reveal.

Dr. Porter already knew I'd cheated, with certainty. He'd recognized the writing. It was from a book he'd read. Written by his college roommate.

This was almost too good and too outrageous a story to be upset about. Almost. I looked into the eyes of a man I respected and found genuine disappointment that I had cheated, put him in the position of failing me, and taken advantage of his trust. If I had simply done the work, I could have written a good paper. We both knew it. Instead, I was forced to see the impact of what I had done. And that it hadn't just affected me.

I was seen. I was caught. It was awful. It was a gift.

Getting away with it rarely turns us around. But getting caught? Getting caught interrupts our movement away from ourselves and away from the truth. It's the invitation to come back, to return, to begin again.

Being seen stings, but it also saves.

17

Moving through It

Back in Seattle, I went to my classes and continued to wrestle. In response to that first question asked of Hagar, I wrote and shared and wrote and shared.

This is where I came from. This is how I came to the end of myself. This is how it all went down. This is how I got here. This is what I remember.

I was still suffering from panic attacks and, admittedly, still acting out in various ways, but something was changing. Time increased between episodes. My acting out was becoming less risky and intense. Certainly I was still causing harm to myself and to others, but I could tell a shift was occurring, even if it was infinitesimal.

I wish I could say I had one of those miraculous thunderbolt sobriety stories. One where you go to your first meeting or hit rock bottom so hard that you're snapped immediately back to reality and never use again. I wanted one of those stories. Desperately so. Instead, my story is a long slog to sobriety—the one day, one hour, one second at a time variety. But over the course of those two years, as I remembered and wrote and shared and finally stopped hiding, healing began one tiny step at a time.

I once heard an aspiring writer ask the showrunner of a popular television show what it took to be successful in Hollywood. The writer was hunting for that one golden nugget of advice, hopeful that the answer would finally reveal the missing piece to her career.

"How do you do it? I mean . . . how *did* you do it?" she pleaded.

The showrunner wondered aloud for a moment. "Well, it's impossible!"

We all laughed. He chuckled too. This wasn't the first time he'd given this answer, and he knew how to deliver it perfectly, landing the joke just so.

The young writer half smiled, unsatisfied.

As the laughter subsided, the sage caught the young woman's eyes, and in them perhaps he saw his own earnest self, many years past, asking for a real answer to a very real question.

The room quieted, feeling the weight of this connection. Like Luke and Obi-Wan standing in the desert. The showrunner met the young writer's stare.

"But . . . you just keep chipping away at the thing that feels impossible, until one day it doesn't," he said at last.

Close friends of mine lost their young daughter several years back. Katie was a gifted painter and a fearless artist. She buzzed with life. One afternoon, while she was driving to work, her brain suffered a catastrophic aneurysm. She was gone before the car even veered off the road. It was a horrible loss.

Katie's dad, Scott, sat across from me and caught his breath from telling the tale once again for a short documentary film I was making about their experience. "People ask you, 'How do you get over it? How do you get over such a loss? How do you get over the pain?' And I tell them, plainly, you don't. You don't get over it. You go *through* it," he said.

I wasn't going to get over my abuse. I wasn't going to get over my addiction. I wasn't going to find some golden nugget of truth that would somehow change my life in an instant. The only way out of the cave was to go through the hurt and the questions and the pain and memories. And as I did, somehow, someway, the impossible began to feel possible. Imperceptible, incremental clicks forward eventually added up and began to feel like progress.

Like real life might be possible.

Even for me.

My time in Seattle was coming to an end. My mom, brother, and Margaret flew out for graduation to mark this unlikely accomplishment with me. This time I didn't march across the stage feeling like I'd gotten away with something. This time I had earned it. I had turned in every assignment, showed up for every exam, written every paper myself, and even figured out how to participate in practicum. For my efforts, I was invited to deliver a speech at the graduation ceremony.

I chose a passage from Romans 8 to frame my talk:

We know that the whole creation has been groaning as in the pains of childbirth right up to the present time. Not only so, but we ourselves, who have the firstfruits of the Spirit, groan inwardly as we wait eagerly for our adoption to sonship, the redemption of our bodies. For in this hope we were saved. But hope that is seen is no hope at all. Who hopes for what they already have? But if we hope for what we do not yet have, we wait for it patiently. (vv. 22–25)

Looking out at a collection of faces that either had known me my whole life or had sat with and seen me while I told them my life's story, I spoke about what it felt like to wait in eager expectation for something new. About being on the precipice of creation while still feeling the cursed ground grabbing us around the ankles, trying to keep us in our place. I spoke about leaning forward into the unknown with the hope that on the other side of this there really is something new. And that I was proof.

In all my Bible learning I'd come to understand that this passage from Romans wasn't so much about heaven but about the blood and guts and sweat and dirt of being fully human. Of living with hope in something still to come. Something you can't quite grasp but you know is waiting for you. Of living with hope that the impossible miracle you can feel in your bones is just outside the cave. As I spoke, inviting my colleagues into this next, new thing, I realized I was inviting myself into something as well. Those living words invited me to consider that this ending in Seattle was merely a blip in my unfolding story. A moment of resolve, surely. A moment of triumph, yes. But this was not the finale.

Too often, this is where we stop telling the story in the Christian tradition. We stop at the victory. The supposed conquest. The good guy gives the big speech, and we roll the credits. It feels so good to leave it all on a high note and not have to wrestle with the complications of life that come after.

We can claim victory and new life, but then we must live it.

Hagar answered the question of her past, just as the man left the cave. While it would be convenient to simply end their stories there and wrap them up with a bow, that is not what happened. It is not the truth. It is not the whole story. Hagar's journey only became more complicated and harder to reconcile after she spoke with the angel of the Lord. Sure, the man made it outside the cave, but then he had to decide what to do with his newfound freedom. And yes, I made it through grad school. I crawled through the stories that maimed and marked me. I came through the valley of the shadow of death, but now I had to figure out how to live.

Hardly knowing where to begin, I hearkened back to my learnings as a maker. It seemed the only way I could understand the miracle of my life now was the same way I'd come to interpret the foundations of my work as an artist, which was through the lenses of creativity and imagination. And by now, these had been cracked wide open, revealing more than I could have ever dreamed.

Creativity isn't magic or a word set aside to describe artists. Creativity is a way of thinking and living differently. And imagination isn't merely playing pretend or blue-sky thinking. Imagination is the practice of creating new possibilities. It all started to make a new kind of sense to me as the creative world of my art collided with a creative understanding of time.

Early in our first semester with Dan, he stepped up to the whiteboard and sketched out three words as he explained that we tend to see time as linear.

PAST → *PRESENT* → *FUTURE*

But if we were to look at time with a bit more creativity and imagination, we might better understand the way we *experience* time and the way that time affects us. Inverting the last two words, he told us that while we think time is moving in a linear fashion, we actually experience it like this:

PAST → *FUTURE* → *PRESENT*

Thus, the way we *interpret* the past is how we *imagine* the future. And how we imagine the *future* defines how we *live* in the present.

As I gave my graduation talk, it was all becoming clear to me. I finally understood what all the remembering was for and why my relationship to my past was the key.

As we've all heard Dan say a million times, "The past is the easiest thing to change." But if that is true, what do we change? The narrative itself? Do we pretend our fathers were not so vicious? Pretend our homes were not so crazy? Pretend our world in America is not so unjust? What Dan's hyperbole is arguing is that we have more power to change our past than we do our present or our future. And I believe he's right. I believe the crazy guy who started this place is telling the truth. Or at least that it's true for me. Of course, we cannot change the nature of our stories. Even a rip in the space-time continuum cannot alter that. But what we can change is the *meaning* of the narrative. And in so doing, we can begin to hope, groaning in eager expectation for what is to come, based on a transformed understanding of what happened in the past.

Looking out at my fellow classmates, at the faces of those who had taught me kindness, I attempted to reciprocate by reciting what I'd learned:

Friends, if faith is a memory of the goodness of God in the past, then hope is faith for the future. The nature of hope, as we've learned, is imagination and an invitation to create what is not yet. It is the opportunity for imagination to take you into a kind of risk that terrifies but tells the truth.

And so let us hope, let us anticipate with agony, knowing the path will be filled with disillusionment and disappointment. No wonder the poor in spirit are to be blessed. So, as we wait in eager expectation for the now and the not yet, be encouraged by the title of that first class that kicked all of our butts.

My friends, let faith, the memory of goodness, solidify you. Let hope get you into all kinds of trouble. And let them both ferry you into the realm of what it means to love.

I'd spent a lifetime incorrectly interpreting my past. I'd believed what I thought those old narratives meant about me, about my life, about my future, as well as my present. But Dan was right. And now I had the experience to prove it. I was so thankful I'd found the courage to face those stories in community so I could begin to engage their real meanings. The work had made a way for me to imagine a new future that was just starting to unfold.

18

Tin Man

Now that I'd officially graduated, I was contemplating signing up for a recovery week that was scheduled to take place just before I was to leave Seattle. It was a concentrated time of therapeutic work for sexual abuse survivors. For five days, I would stay in a house on an island off the coast of Seattle and work through my story. I hesitated to register since I figured that I'd already done the work—two years' worth, in fact.

I'd told the stories out loud in groups and in therapy, and I'd written thousands of pages of tales. What else could I discover that I hadn't already?

Yet Dan's words rang loud: "Every time you tell a story, more than likely there will be new data, or a reclaiming of memories, that you didn't hear in the first telling."

I relented and figured it couldn't hurt. A fresh recollection of goodness might be a lovely capstone to end my time in Seattle.

Famous last words.

I packed my bag and rode the ferry across Puget Sound to Bainbridge Island.

Awaiting me on the other side was a ragtag group of men. Some were divorced, some were previously incarcerated, and some were awaiting word on whether they'd be losing their jobs or worse. I was the youngest of the lot by a decade. In between delicious meals, runs on the beach at dawn, and teachings by Dan around the nature of abuse and addiction, we each spent individual time with a therapist. One hour a day for five days in a row, telling our stories.

On the last day, I was dreading my final appointment. What else was there to say? I'd pored over every inch of every story I could possibly remember. I was going to have to come up with something to say; I couldn't just sit there. While I'd proved I could handle three minutes of silence, there was no way I could manage sixty.

As I sat down, a familiar sense greeted me, not unlike the blinking cursor egging me on to tell on myself. But this felt bigger somehow, like the last bits of something trying to break through. Like warm lava trying to bubble up to the surface and force itself into the light. I was two years into this new song and dance and should have known better. But instead, I attempted to stuff whatever truth was trying to be born.

"Blaine, can I ask? What brought you here?" the therapist asked plainly.

"The ferry," I said with a smile.

He smiled back.

Just as I thought I'd secured my defenses with a joke, a memory I'd not had in some time slipped through a crack. I tried to grab the recollection by its foggy tail but couldn't stuff it back in time. My confidence fell, and my cocky gaze dissolved into a blank stare.

"What is it?"

"Nothing."

"You're somewhere else."

Silence.

I squinted out the window. Dark clouds were forming in the sky, like round billows of smoke.

"Blaine, what *story* brought you here?" he said, taking a different route.

The memory quietly trickled out from its hiding place again, warm and sulfurous. I swallowed hard, shaking my head, pushing down whatever buried fragment of the past was starting to come into view.

"I've already told it. So many times. I've written it. Spoken it. Made art about it!"

By the last sentence, I was practically yelling.

Meeting my anger with laser-focused kindness, he said, "I want you to tell me the story you haven't told."

This time the heat felt like it was coming from some invisible core. From deep inside me, trying with all its might to connect me to a truth I'd always struggled to believe: I will be taken care of.

This truth rode on the back of the notion that goodness and wholeness were there—somewhere, somehow—and that if I wanted, I could finally let go of the shame I'd been attempting to keep smothered and hidden. I could finally let go of this idea that *I was bad* and maybe, just maybe, begin to embrace the fact that care and kindness were woven all the way through my story. It became clear that if I wanted to be free, I'd have to tell the story. When would I learn?

I tightened my jaw and locked my voice. But bright holy light kept on burning, refining, revealing. My shame blazed, escaping from the hidden space I'd been stuffing it into for years—threatening to expose all I'd tried so hard to keep in the dark. The waves I could see from my seat crashed against the shore, goading me. *Tell it.* I was sitting on a lit fuse, and everything was about to explode.

FINE!

I'LL TELL!

I'll tell . . .

My body loosened and I took a deep breath.

"I should have known better," I said softly.

As I spoke, the fire within rushed upward. The dam holding it all back was gone. Hot tears ran down my face.

The therapist held the moment with me, and then he gently said, "Tell me more."

Turns out there was one more memory I had to unearth.

In Chicago, three years before coming to Seattle, while I'd been having those panic attacks that were taking me to the hospital, I'd also been going to a men's recovery group for sex addicts in the basement of Margaret's suburban megachurch.

We sat in circles and spoke anonymously. We told our truths and told on ourselves. We made our affirmations and drank all the bad coffee. One evening, a man named Ed came to deliver a fiery speech about the power we could have over our addictions. That there was more to it than simply saying no to sin and lust.

After we'd finished our affirmations, I waited in line to talk to him. When he shook my hand, some part of me could already tell what was going on. But at the time, I didn't have the tools to understand it. One of my best friends, Steve, always says that kids are excellent at intuition but awful at interpretation. While this kid could certainly intuit something was off, I wasn't yet able to decipher it.

Ed was the head of pastoral care at the megachurch. He was a deeply respected man who'd suffered his own abuse and been redeemed in all the ways necessary to work at a church of that size and influence. We began meeting regularly. In our meetings, we imagined the good that could be done if we combined his research and understanding of addiction with my creative spirit. *Was this the next big thing in sex addiction recovery?* we asked ourselves. *How many lives could be changed?*

After almost a year of meeting and dreaming, he suggested a technique he'd discovered that essentially erased any power addiction might have over someone. It involved bringing a trusted person into your compulsion, not just by telling them your story but by inviting them into your vices. If your proclivities took you to adult theaters or DVD shops or at-home viewing, then this trusted mentor must be brought in. Doing this with the right person, in the right way, could break the bonds of addiction completely.

But I needn't rush into such a big decision, he told me. And then he quoted Scripture, "Like Jesus said, you must ask yourself: 'Do I want to be well?'"

Margaret and I were together at the time—albeit still on and off and nearly always dependent on my own addiction cycle. When I brought Ed's idea to her, we prayed about it, which is what our tradition teaches when faced with a big life moment. We were eager for healing. The idea itself felt so bizarre. But this was supposed to be an experimental, innovative process, and Ed was optimistic about the potential.

And despite our shared hesitation, I eventually said, "Yes. Of course. I want to be well."

One bright summer afternoon, on a weekend that his wife was out of town, Ed took the train into the city to meet me after a matinee performance of a show I was doing at the Chicago Shakespeare Theater. I drove him back to my apartment, where we sat in the living room to pray together about what this time could be, and then we were off.

But before we headed out on our addiction-altering adventure, I grabbed a cardboard box I'd hidden in my closet. It contained all the DVDs and magazines I'd been looking forward to throwing away at the end of our journey. It seemed clear to me that if this was going to work, I'd no longer need the box of porn to keep me company. I was going to be healed. I was going to be well.

We'd planned a sacred and profane trek that would take us on an odyssey throughout the city to all the adult bookstores and video shops I'd been visiting since coming to live in Chicago.

We pulled up to the first one and I stopped the car.

"That one?" He pointed.

I nodded.

Ed put his hand on my shoulder and began to pray for me to be released from my addiction. I folded my hands and closed my eyes. My heart picked up speed as the sun bounced off the hood of my Saturn, warming my face. I felt safe, almost serene. The warmth spread to my whole body, and I breathed it in as deeply as I could.

For the first time in a long time, I felt at ease and filled with a real sense of hope. Maybe something holy was happening. Maybe I could be done with this once and for all.

His prayer ended, and he said, "Amen."

I exhaled, letting go of years of shame, and started to put the car into drive. But his hand was still on my shoulder, and he gripped it tighter.

"Now, let's go inside."

The glow vanished from my body, replaced immediately by a cold dark blackness. I froze. How could I not have known?

Ed continued, "Blaine, you can't really be done with it until you invite someone *in*. Let's do it together."

I wanted to scream, "No!" I wanted to cry. I wanted to run. But I couldn't find a single word. I felt hollow and stuck. The years of hurt that had been so sweetly ushered out of my body mere moments ago flooded back in an instant, filling me to the brim, weighing down any lightness I'd felt. No longer buoyed by hope, I was drowning once again in shame.

We spent the rest of that afternoon in seedy DVD shops and peepshow joints, sitting in tiny booths thick with the scent of chlorine and sadness as fleshy images flickered. As I heard moans and groans in one ear, Ed whispered prayers in the other. He prayed for light to come in the darkness, for me to be released from my addiction, for my healing and wholeness. This mix of holy horror was too much to take. My body went numb.

And I disappeared.

As our trek wound down, I grew more and more anxious by the second. Whatever hope for freedom I'd felt hours earlier had disappeared, and I was desperate for our experiment to come to an end.

I glanced at the clock in the car, realizing, thankfully, that Ed's train back to the suburbs would be arriving soon.

Even though the sun was at its most golden hour, the breeze fresh and clear, and the sky a perfect blue, I felt more like I was navigating the car through a Hagar-like fog. I just wanted to be free of this man. As we headed west, back toward the train station near my apartment, the sun pushed through my windshield and tried once more to heat my body. To remind me that truth and goodness and wholeness did still exist. Yet while I could feel the sunny air on my skin, it couldn't compete with the coolness within.

I pulled up underneath the tracks. "Next stop: Damen." The voice blared overhead. I knew there were just a few minutes before Ed's train would pull into the station. I thanked him for his time, saying how I hoped it could be the end of this for me. By now, I was shaking.

With a wry look, he sat in the passenger seat, still as stone. I wanted him to leave. Then I remembered the box I'd taken from my apartment. I wanted to be done with its contents, and I hoped mentioning it would be enough to get him out of my car. I wanted this day to be over. I needed Ed gone. But most of all, I wanted to be clean and clear of these mementos. I really did want to be well.

"So, I, uh—brought a box of . . . stuff. I thought maybe we could throw it away together. Kind of a sendoff," I said, gesturing to the green dumpster over my shoulder.

He smiled warmly.

"I don't need to go yet. And you're right. It feels like there's one last step."

I braced myself.

The doors clicked shut on the train above. As it clacked away on the electric tracks toward the city, I could hear the outbound train approaching.

"Your place is so close. Let's go back and watch some of it together," he said.

He conjured a fake thought to himself, then continued, "Yes. You're right, Blaine. That's what I meant by inviting someone in. I'm sensing that's the last step."

I exited my body and floated through the hood of my car, looking around at everyone else going about their day. A man loosened his tie and hummed to the song in his headphones before bounding down the steps of the platform. A gaggle of teenage girls burst into laughter. A woman in a brown uniform dropped off a package at the liquor store across the street. The sidewalks buzzed with energy. I was envious of everyone's seemingly effortless ability to be at peace, going about normal things. I ached with jealousy, wishing to be one of them. I didn't want to be me. Stuck in another terrifying story.

I slammed back into my body and as my soul met the seat, my entire car seemed to shake with resolve.

"No. I think you should go home, Ed. Right now."

Though he was still smiling, I could see a flicker of fear deep in his eyes.

"Thank you for this time today, Blaine. I'll be praying for you. See you next week."

He got out and I watched his lanky body ascend the steps. From below I could see his shadowed feet making their way across the platform. I eyed them until they disappeared into the train.

"Next stop: California."

The train pulled away, removing the cloud shading my car from the setting sun. The orangey glow filled the space, again attempting to comfort and soothe, to tell me everything was going to be OK. But it was no use.

Trembling, I got out of my car and opened my trunk, revealing my box of goodies. I leaned over to lug it out with the intention of emptying it but was overcome with a spark of ick piercing my belly. I ran to the dumpster and emptied my stomach instead. I gripped the side of the rusty metal bin and heaved again.

I wiped my mouth and straightened. My eyes, bleary and bloodshot, caught the last glimpse of the train ferrying Ed until it vanished from view. I swallowed the acid aftertaste, walked back to my trunk, and slammed it shut. Night fell as I sped home. And under the cover of darkness, I lugged the box back up the two flights of stairs and gently set it back in my closet.

The following week, I warily arrived at Ed's office for our scheduled meeting only to find it locked with the lights off. I called his number but only got a busy signal. An email to him asking if I'd gotten the day wrong returned an autoreply saying that Ed no longer worked at the church.

Turns out I was not the only one.

The next few weeks were a blur of appointments with elders from the church who asked to hear my story. Because of the "severity of the abuse," my case was put on the proverbial back burner. Apparently, Ed had gained further access with the others. For my trouble, I was given a small stipend to use toward counseling and some check-ins on my progress along the way.

A handful of months after Ed's experiment ended, I landed in Seattle. Two years and some change after that, here I was, sitting on an island as the story that had brought me here finally came spilling out. Thunder rolled. Sheets of rain thin as glass struck the salty sea. And along with the rain outside, I wept. How, in these two years of storytelling, had I forgotten the story that literally sent me here?

As I heaved out deep sobs, I let my body release the shame and grief of the shadows I'd been hiding for so long.

I wept for the shadows Ed made for me. For the ways he had carefully—masterfully, even—twisted the words of Jesus and used them to ensnare me. For the ways he had abused the authority given to him by the church, subtly asking me to ignore my own warning lights and trust blindly instead. For the ways he had distorted my deep longing to be well and used it against me only to bring me more harm. As the tears came, I realized they weren't just grieving one untold story but all the stories, all the memories, all the darkness.

I wept for what M and S had done to me all those years ago. I wept for the generational shame that had been placed on my shoulders by my dad. I wept for the lost little boy who needed to know he wasn't alone. I wept for the ways I'd fashioned shadows for myself, and I wept for the shadows I'd cast for the innumerable others along the way. Friends, partners, strangers, Margaret. I wept for the darkness I'd hidden in and the darkness I'd asked others to hide in with me. I wept for the darkness I'd been shown and for the darkness I'd shown others.

And there it was.

This . . .

This . . .

This . . . was where I'd come from. This was what I was meant to remember. This was the catalog of stories from the past I was meant to change. To see differently. Whose meanings I was meant to transform.

On the final day of the retreat, our ragamuffin crew was gathered together and informed that we'd be driven to the neighboring town and dropped off with a twenty-dollar bill. The money was to be used to purchase an item that represented the week at the retreat, a totem of sorts. We piled into a black Suburban and drove through the rain into the quaint downtown. I'd forgotten places like this existed in America. Without a Walmart in sight, we split up and wandered through old-timey drugstores, souvenir shops, and vintage establishments.

The rain stopped, and the glory of Seattle at sunset was showing off. Mist rose from the cobblestones, glowing with all kinds of sweetness. Twinkles of light dripped from the eaves—rainy remnants bursting into tiny explosions of sun as they hit the ground. The sky's pinky hue wrapped around me like an old-school fabric softener ad, reminding me yet again that everything would be OK.

I stepped into a little antique shop, and a tiny brass bell dinged to alert the clerk of my presence. An old woman wearing an apron and a bent pair of gold, wireframe bifocals appeared. A pencil tied up her silver hair into a messy bun. She was every single small-town shop owner from every single '80s movie I'd ever seen.

"Looking for something?" she asked.

I cracked a smile. "You have no idea."

"Well, I hope you find it."

"Me too."

And with that she disappeared into the back, leaving me to wander alone through the piles of curios and knickknacks. Rusty red wagons. A spotless set of grandma doilies. Yellowed cardstock with penciled-in prices hung delicately from worn strings. But nothing caught my eye.

I started to wonder, with a sense of disappointment and panic, if I was going to have to fake this final exercise. But I wanted to do it. I wanted it to work. I wanted it to work *on me*.

Then, after a few more moments of meandering aimlessly, I saw it. Standing proudly on a shelf a few feet away: a hand-painted figurine of the Tin Man from *The Wizard of Oz*.

Of course.

The Wizard of Oz was a funny recurring plot point in my story. Throughout my years as a child actor, I was in *The Wizard of Oz* three times. First, as you'll remember, I was Lollipop Guild Number 2. The second time, I reprised that role at the community theater the next town over. Word had apparently gotten out that I could be trusted to sing and dance with a large lollipop. The third time was as a young teen, and I played the Scarecrow.

But I always wanted to play the Tin Man.

And I almost had my chance.

Halfway through my time at Seattle, I was asked to audition a second tie for the Broadway production of *Wicked*. I'd already met the director and auditioned once, and now they wanted to fly me to NYC for a callback. Although they'd initially gone another direction, they wanted to see me again. The audition was for the role of Boq, the character who eventually becomes the Tin Man.

I hadn't been acting or auditioning for over a year, so the call shocked me. It was a dream opportunity and literally everything I'd hoped for up until the panic attack that graciously wrecked my life. But if they offered me the role, it would mean leaving school a year early and diving back into my old life. Somehow, though, I knew I wasn't done with Seattle. Or, put more plainly, Seattle wasn't done with me. As much as it hurt and as much as it went against the life I'd spent over a decade building, I knew I wasn't ready to go. I guess that's the thing about transformation. As you change, you are able to make different decisions. You can see new paths forward where there used to be none. So, as a surprise to even myself, I declined the audition.

This knowing wink from my story now found me face-to-face with a Tin Man figurine in an antique shop in a city that is lovingly known as the Emerald City. The irony wasn't lost on me.

If you don't know much about the story of the Tin Man, let me fill you in. You see, he doesn't start out the way we see him in the movie we all know and love: frozen in the forest, eking out the words, "Oil can!" Instead, his origin story is a bit darker, and the character has rather humble beginnings as a simple woodsman by the name of Nick Chopper.

The story goes that Nick falls in love with the servant girl of a very old woman. But the old woman doesn't want her servant distracted from her work, so she appeals to the Wicked Witch of the East, the one with the green face who eventually yells, "I'll get you, my pretty!" When the old woman begs for a spell to be cast on Nick Chopper, the Wicked Witch obliges. For the price of a couple cows and a sheep, a hex is placed on Nick's ax.

The rest of the tale is a bit gruesome, for as time goes on, the enchanted ax periodically chops off one of Nick's limbs. Fortunately, these seemingly horrific accidents don't have too much of an effect on Nick, because each time a body part is lopped off, he simply replaces the missing limb with one made of tin. This goes on for years until, eventually, his body is made entirely of metal.

At this point it may seem like the spell had worked its dreadful magic (who could love a tin man, after all?), but the final macabre act is just beginning. Nick starts to realize that his emotions are dulling. Without a real flesh-and-blood body, his heart cannot survive. And without his heart, he loses his ability to love. Finally, his feelings for the servant girl have all but disappeared.

While it took some time, evil eventually won.

As I held this figurine in my hands, wiping dust from its base, staring at its tin physique, the connection was clear. Over the years, there were so many ways I'd participated in chopping off my own limbs, so many times I'd felt like the only things left of me were a metal body and a barely beating heart. I'd dismembered myself more times than I'd care to admit.

I stared at the figurine. This was my totem.

Later that night, we finished our last meal together as a group, then we went around the table, taking turns sharing the reasons behind the various trinkets we'd chosen in town earlier that day.

Gripping the Tin Man figurine, I shared the story of Nick and the ways his story spoke to mine. After we'd all had our turn, Dan rose from the table and told us there'd be one more movement to our time together: communion.

As Dan spoke, it all started to make sense. The cave. The hero. The flickering shadows. The push toward the light. The enslaved Egyptian woman. The running away. The being seen. That first question the angel asked of Hagar. Oh, and Jesus.

"On the night Jesus was betrayed, surrounded by His closest friends, He took a loaf of bread, broke it, and said: 'This is My body, which is for you; do this in remembrance of Me.' And then later that night, in that same way, after supper He took the cup, saying, 'This cup is the new covenant in My blood; do this, whenever you drink it, in remembrance of Me.'"

From Munchkin Land to Seattle to the first century, my mind traveled back to Jesus as He sat around the table with His comrades that night. He knew that in a matter of hours He would be betrayed and then broken. He named it Himself.

Looking into the eyes of His friends, He says, "Like this bread, like this wine, I will be broken, dismembered, and poured out."

And then He says, perhaps, the most shocking thing of all. "Do this in remembrance of Me."

What is He asking, really? Jesus is facing His own very human demise, knowing what His friends don't yet know: His death will be surrounded in a holy mystery. If Jesus's life was meant to reveal God's character, so then, too, would His death. Perhaps He was inviting them to remember that the tearing apart He was about to endure would be so they could be made whole again. That God was good enough and big enough to pull life from even the most lifeless ashes.

As I watched Dan dip bread into the wine and pass the simple cup around the table, Jesus's choice of words pulled me in. His invitation was to *remember Him*, as He was about to *remember us*. These living words from this ancient text spun me. But one got stuck on repeat, running round and round in a kind of cosmic loop in my mind.

Remember. Remember. *Remember.*

The word wound itself around my heart like a tetherball, tighter and tighter, until suddenly it unraveled, whirring itself loose. Its letters burst open, exposing their insides. I watched as the word reformed into something entirely new. A tiny hyphen lovingly placed changed its meaning altogether.

Re-member.

This word wasn't just conjuring a vague notion of the past but was invoking something fleshier and more rich, wilder and more active. We weren't just talking about the wispy idea of remembrance any longer but the explosive action of *remaking*.

Re-member.

Put back together.

Make whole again.

"Remember Me . . . as I want to *re-member you*."

Christ allowed Himself to be torn apart so that we might be made whole in the places where we have been dismembered by the shadows of evil and by the shadows of our own doing.

That night I took the elements sitting next to my little Tin Man. As I ate and drank and cried again, new questions bubbled up.

Which parts of myself still need to be put back together?

Where do I need to be made whole again?

What would it look like for the power of the crucified and risen Christ to re-member me?

And perhaps most potent of all:

What would it look like to see all the re-membering that has already occurred?

My mind floated back to earlier that morning, to my final moments with my therapist. After I'd finished telling the story of Ed, the story I'd forgotten to tell, I wiped tears from my eyes and wondered aloud, "How could I have forgotten?"

He spoke kindly and sweetly. "You weren't ready. You weren't ready to remember."

Looking out at this table of men who were telling their own stories, I smiled through new tears as a powerful revelation formed. As I remembered my story, I was re-membering myself.

Where have you come from? What do you remember?
The questions that had launched my journey to Seattle and that had kept me coming back to the truth all this time had not let me down. I thought of Dan in the Korean church, the battlefield of the practicum rooms, and the countless hours spent writing and speaking the stories I thought I could hide from.

Where have you come from? What do you remember?
These questions allowed me to see that the work of remembering is the work of wholeness. The work of freedom. The real work of creativity. Of changing the meaning of the past to imagine a new future.

And I learned, too, that timing really is everything. Because sometimes we simply aren't ready. Not ready to remember—to recall the actual memory of the past. And not ready to re-member—to be formed into something new.

Until, of course, we are.

19

Golden Possibility

All the world's a stage, as Shakespeare so famously wrote, and while the stage had once been the only place I could imagine possibility, I was now seeing it in my actual life.

Writer Peter Block explains it like this:

> Possibility can work on us only when we have come to terms with our story. Whatever we hold as our story, which is our version of the past, and from which we take our identity becomes the limitation to living into a new possibility.[1]

In everyone's life, there comes a time when the old way of doing things—the way that kept you sane and safe for a time—no longer works. It is an unwanted reckoning where you face the reality that the old way, which once felt like life, now leads only to death. And until you can re-member your past, you will always be limited by the version of a story you believe cannot be changed.

It can. But you must decide. Are you ready? Or, in the words of Jesus, "Do you want to be well?" I hope you are. I hope you do.

Be forewarned, though, because the stories that are your darkest, the ones that bear some of the greatest shame, the ones that you have not been willing to enter, let alone tell, have elements of kindness and of presence and goodness that you cannot even imagine. And if my tale is anything like yours (and I assure you it is) you have no idea the golden possibilities hidden in your story.

I sat on the ferry facing east, headed back to Seattle after my week on Bainbridge Island. I was exhausted, but grateful. My two-year odyssey had come to an end. I'd named and faced the taunting shadows dancing on the wall as I finally exited the cave. I wrestled honestly with Hagar's first question. I tried to let it all sink into my bones.

But this moment of reprieve was brief. My mind wandered to the future, to what sounded like a new countdown from mission control. Just as I was about to be relaunched across the country, Hagar's next great question arose like the skyline of the Emerald City coming into view.

Where are you going?

PART THREE

Where Are You Going?

20

Seeing the Light

I had a new job and Margaret waiting for me back in Chicago. Not knowing how I was going to take this entire experience and fashion it into new life, I went back to Plato.

When Plato told his allegory of the cave, he did so through dialogue. Classic philosopher's move, if you ask me. Instead of a simple narrative, the story was told through questions between a teacher named Socrates and his student, Glaucon. Toward the end of the allegory, as our hero comes to the edge of the cave, finally meeting the light he's been seeking for so very long, Socrates asks his pupil a somewhat rhetorical question about what is unfolding.

SOCRATES

Would not the one who had been dragged like this feel, in the process, pain and rage? And when he got into the sunlight,

159

wouldn't his eyes be filled with the glare, and wouldn't he thus be unable to see any of the things that are now revealed to him as the unhidden?

GLAUCON

He would not be able to do that at all, at least not right away.[1]

How infuriating. How defeating. After all that work to get out of the darkness, shouldn't the light feel easy breezy lemon squeezy? Of course, I was discovering that anything new takes time. And while I wanted the light without the pain of its glare, it was not possible—at least not right away.

21

Wanting New Things

Once again, I have a story to tell that begins with me in my underwear.

A few months before seminary graduation, I woke late on a Saturday. After the obligatory morning trip to the bathroom, I wandered into the living room to find one of my roommates and his recent fiancée cuddled up on the couch. She barely registered my attire (or lack thereof).

"Morning, Blaine," she said, without looking up from her phone.

I scratched my head and stretched. Yawning, I lazily asked, "What are you guys up to?"

"Going to look at wedding bands," my roommate muttered, also not looking up from his phone.

"Can I come?"

I surprised even myself by the question. I'd long declared my intention to remain a bachelor. I was hopelessly devoted to an untethered life on my own. Free to do whatever I wanted, whenever I wanted. But as I was learning, living untethered was not always what it promised to be. And doing whatever I wanted, whenever I wanted, did not actually get me what I wanted.

As I continued to change my relationship to my past, I slowly started to twist myself out of the mold I'd carefully poured myself into. I was starting to imagine my future differently. I was starting to let myself change my mind. To let myself want and long for new things. Things that might bring me new life. More life. *Truer-to-me* life.

So there, as I stood in the living room in my underwear while my two friends scrolled their phones looking for the nearest jeweler, a thought appeared as clear as that first sunny day in Seattle: *I need to marry Margaret.*

We had managed to find our way through the first year of long distance while I was in grad school. Miraculously, although we were undergoing massive shifts individually, we still longed to work through it all together. We had a new language. We carried new insights. We were moving increasingly toward integrity. The best parts of ourselves made sense together. Our conversations gradually shifted from tired old loops to the possibility of futures stretched out side by side.

While at school I'd been working on various marketing and video campaigns to earn money where I could. After cobbling together three months of savings from odd jobs as well as a little bit of student loan money I'd siphoned off, I cashed out. Literally. I'd always been told by my dad that you'd get a better deal if you brought cash to a store. It gave you more negotiating power, he said. I took Jarrod with me for support. After I'd picked the stone and the setting, the lady across the counter named the price.

"Well . . .," I said, flashing a coy smile and side-winking my pal. I pulled my money from the crinkled envelope, fanned out the bills, triumphantly plopped them on the glass counter, and continued, "I brought cash!"

"Oh good!" she shot back. "That makes it easier."

With that, she scooped up every dollar I had to my name while I watched in horror as the stack disappeared into the register behind her.

In my nervous excitement, I'd forgotten to negotiate.

22

Saying "I Do"

A few weeks later I flew to Chicago with a ring in my pocket.

Whenever Margaret and I had allowed ourselves to day-dream about marriage, it was always in the context of *making*. What else could a marriage between two artists be? So, when I proposed, that is what we did. Late at night, on the empty stage of the old auditorium in the megachurch that had been such a big part of our stories, I carefully mapped out an art project for us to make—a painting on a giant canvas. It was all a ruse, of course, because as the last song of the curated playlist boom-ing from the loudspeakers, which I'd begged one of the tech people to let me use, faded, I got down on one knee and asked Margaret if she would marry me. If she would be my partner in an ongoing art project, endeavoring to *make*, together.

A life, a family, dinners, babies, a home, friends, messes, mis-takes, and on and on.

We'd already weathered a lot of heartache. Individually. And, sadly, together. We had created destruction. Yet we'd also expe-rienced an enormous amount of grace and healing and growth.

Just enough, in fact, to believe a new future was possible. That we could build something different from what we'd already tried. Different from what we'd known. Different from what we'd been taught. We had managed to find enough faith to propel us into hope, and that hope was now moving us into love.

She said yes.

Terrified but excited, we planned a wedding. And as the sun was setting on a late summer night, we exchanged our vows. It was a wild act of hope. And it was beautiful. We invited David, a friend and fellow student from Seattle, to sing and play guitar at the ceremony. And rather than the standard "Wedding March," we asked him to play the old hymn "How Great Thou Art," as Margaret walked down the aisle.

Softly, he began. "Oh Lord, my God! When I, in awesome wonder . . ."

When the strings of his guitar echoed throughout the cavernous space, strumming the big chords leading into the chorus, the doors of the auditorium flung wide open, and Margaret appeared.

I was a puddle.

And then, just like that, we were official.

Husband and wife.

I believe something holy happens in the exchange of vows. Holy, not magical. Our hard pasts were not erased. Our aches and wounds were not vanquished. We were still us. But now we had promised to go forward together. Partners in the remembering. Partners in dreaming up new futures. Partners in the courageous act of love. Partners in the creative act of changing our pasts and making a life as two becoming one. We discovered that there truly was safety in numbers and great relief in knowing we didn't have to try alone.

There were, of course, growing pains. The irritations and shocks that come when you live with someone for the first time. One night I found Margaret hiding in the bathroom, crying. When I was finally able to coax her into telling me what was wrong, she whispered, "It's just. It's just . . . you're here all the time. I know you live here now, or whatever, but you never go home."

I looked into the eyes of my new wife and saw her own story dancing in her eyes. She was an only child until she was fourteen. Turns out, while she was incredibly giving, she wasn't great at sharing. And marriage meant so much sharing. Plus, there wasn't exactly space for her to do all the weird Margaret stuff she did alone, like pretending she was Russian, or staging epic plays, or bawling on the floor under dining room tables while listening to Whitney Houston. It was hard for her to do all the singing and the strange accents and the twirling about when there was another human around. She cried some more. And then we laughed.

And then we tried to have sex, which brought about even more growing pains. We were working through the practice of truly leaving our families of origin. Combining our vastly opposite sexual histories. Arguing about money. Engaging in the push and pull of desperately wanting to hide and desperately wanting to be seen. And on and on and on.

We held on to what, at times, seemed like only a dot of hope.

For Margaret's birthday I bought her a simple necklace, a tiny sterling silver dot suspended on a sterling silver chain. To remember. A symbol that, no matter what, there was a dot of hope to reach for. And boy, did we have to reach for it.

We needed the kind of hope my classmates and I had talked about nearly ad nauseam at seminary. But we needed it now, in real life.

Hope is a memory of what is to come. It is faith for the future.

In defiance of suffering, hope allows us to dream and desire. But hope requires a certain perseverance, a daily sacrifice that often grows best through disaster—something we were.

Margaret and I realized that hope would require a kind of daily tending. We would have to be defiant. And we would have to learn to hold the tension of our ambivalence.

You know what else hope requires? Creativity.

Building a life together from our broken stories, a shared life that had started so tumultuously and already carried plenty of pain, was going to take serious imagination. The idea of real intimacy scared us both, in different ways. Margaret, for example, dragged her feet for over a year and a half before legally changing her last name, because then, she thought, we would be *really* married. It didn't help that when she finally summoned the nerve, the clerk at the DMV told her not to do it. "Nobody stays married," she said. "Mark my words. You'll want your own name."

Beyond that, Margaret also struggled to find her voice. She'd learned to keep her big feelings, her big emotions, her big needs quiet, hidden, and small. Although she desperately hoped to be noticed and seen, she found herself almost speechless when it came to naming those things aloud. And so, those important pieces of herself went unnoticed and unspoken.

And I, too, found myself driving away what I so deeply wanted. I dove into work and I had the perfect new job to hide in.

When I returned from Seattle, I intended to return to acting. I figured we'd live in downtown Chicago, Margaret would commute out to the suburbs and continue working at our church, and I'd call my agent to start lining up auditions. But as we settled into our new life together, we both sensed the pull to take risks in different directions. Margaret was accepted into a screenwriting program, and I decided to apply for a position at the church. And in short order, everything we thought we knew was going to happen had flipped itself on its head. We would live in the suburbs. I would work at the church. And Margaret would take on the freelance life. I mean, if we were going to *make it up*, why not *make it new?*

While the leap to working on a church staff was a big one, strangely it made sense. I had a theater degree, a professional life as an actor and director, and now a master's degree in theology and culture, all of which seemed like just the kind of mix needed to produce memorable weekly services meant to fill a seven-thousand-seat evangelical megachurch. An added benefit to being on a church staff was it provided a kind of stability and accountability I'd never experienced before. Having only ever jumped from gig to gig and town to town, I relished the consistency.

And yet it wasn't all rainbows and unicorns and Jesus, as I soon learned that being on a church staff was very different from being a mere member of the flock. For all its good in the world, the church too often screamed its own importance by way of imposing constant urgency, demanding unhealthy boundaries, and requiring ironclad loyalty from its employees.

When I periodically got too afraid or felt too overwhelmed with the constant ask to create, I would act out online, even though I knew it was damaging. While it was so much tamer than what I'd spent a decade doing—thank God—it still wreaked havoc. It still helped me hide. And this marriage wouldn't survive if I spent it hiding.

Margaret and I knew this would be a challenge. We'd done the individual counseling. We'd done the premarital counseling. We'd been working our programs and our stories. And we knew that joining the lives of two codependent adult children of addicts would have its ups and downs. Which is why we decided to forgo any traditional gifts to each other on the day of our wedding. Nothing sweet or sparkly or expensive or sentimental. Instead, we promised that we would go to counseling together, every week, for the first year of our marriage. That was the gift. That was the commitment. To show up, together. To practice the painful work of seeing and being seen, and to invite a trusted professional to bear witness. And, obviously, to help us sort through fights.

The truth is, I think we both secretly hoped something miraculous would happen the day we got married. Something that would magically heal the leftover dynamics we had been reenacting for years.

We felt like we'd made it out of the belly of the beast to even get to this place. Having already fought so hard to emerge from the cave, we longed for the warmth of the sun as we stood on the precipice of our future. Instead, the sun burned like absolute hell.

A lifetime of living in the dark can make the brightness of a new day—of possibility—seem unbearable. But we pressed on. We'd come too far to give up now.

For my part, I just tried to keep moving and keep showing up, even when the hot glow of the sun felt as if it might consume me entirely. Because with a lifetime before us, Margaret and I were just getting started.

As our counselor and good friends reminded me, I was no longer the person who'd left two years ago. I had new data. I had new experiences. I held new truths. I had different tools. I was learning to lean into faith, hope, and yes . . . maybe even love.

23

Radical Imagination and Containers on the Floor

After a long day of work, I made it home to our new apartment—and to a giddy new wife awaiting my arrival. As soon as I was inside, she screamed from the back bedroom.

"Stop! Don't come in. Close your eyes!"

She giggled as she rounded the corner and took my hand, leading me into our front room: a windowless den that had become a moving-in catchall space I'd been desperate for Margaret to organize. I smiled to myself, wondering if this was one of those sexy after-work surprises.

"Open your eyes!" She proudly gestured to a slightly less disheveled array of bins and boxes. "What do you think?!"

Sexy time this was not. Without skipping a beat, I offered my muted praise.

"Nice."

"Nice?!"

"Yeah. Nice."

I flashed back to Seattle. It was the last day of class, and the sign-in sheet had made its way to Joshua, one of my many roommates. As he checked off his name, he shouted out with enormous pride, "Hey look, I've been to every class this semester!"

Our teacher coolly replied, "Congratulations, Mr. Longbrake, on doing exactly what was expected of you." Our professor's apathy had made its way from that classroom in Seattle, across time and space, all the way to our tiny abode in Elgin, Illinois, and into my voice. And I wasn't even done.

"Do you want me to help?" I asked.

"Do I want you to *help*?"

"Yeah. With the boxes."

"I don't need your help, *Blaine*! I already *organized* the boxes!"

"Oh."

With a furious stare, she stormed back to the bedroom.

I'd obviously missed it. I'd been missing it. For some time now. I felt like I was stunted emotionally. Like I couldn't connect correctly. Like I wouldn't let myself. Like I didn't know how—which, as it turned out, was the real truth. I just didn't know how. I'd never really seen a husband and wife work it out.

How was this all going to work?

How were we going to work?

Later that night, I snuck out of bed and made my way back to the den to take another look at Margaret's handiwork. She really had done so much. It just took a little more careful observing than I had been initially willing to do. She had gone through mountains of old stuff, hers and mine. She'd thrown out bags and bags of trash. Sorted piles of like things and organized what was left into manageable piles. It was the un-glamorous, tedious work of putting two lives together. Work that often goes unnoticed but still must be done. As I stared at our two lives stacked on top of each other in clear plastic bins, I wondered if we'd ever really unpack their contents (figuratively and literally) or if we should just keep them stored to ease the packing when the end inevitably came. Like sitting near the exit, just in case. This is what I'd learned, after all.

I snapped myself back from my bleak spiral. I owed my wife an apology. And I owed my marriage my courage and an honest attempt at the creativity and imagination I'd spoken so much about as an artist.

Just days earlier, Margaret had stopped by my office while I was in a meeting. She left a cup of coffee on my desk and this note on my giant whiteboard:

We need radical imagination now more than ever—to conceive of some better, alternative, hopeful future.

She'd been thinking less about our personal lives and more about her desire for a cultural and theological renaissance. She was longing for something pulsing with energy and creativity. Something worth building. Something fervent and bigger than one person. Something new to get swept up in. Something you dive into because you believe in where it will take you and believe in its power to transform.

And in so doing, she'd conjured up the perfect phrase to de-scribe the active work of hope in our own lives. If hope was faith for the future, then this wild, willful believing that something better was possible and the defiant implication that we could be part of birthing it had to be explored.

Whether she'd penned that phrase with a particular discontent within the world at large in mind, or as a direct call toward a better marriage, the phrase stuck. Radical imagination was precisely what we needed.

24

Past. Future. Present.

There can be no hope which does not constitute itself through a *we* and for a *we*. I would be very tempted to say that all hope is at the bottom choral.

Gabriel Marcel, *Tragic Wisdom and Beyond*

Surrounded by the boxes of our lives, I tried to choose hope, to radically imagine something new in our newlywed apartment that night. I recognized that we, too, were merely containers. We held stories and scraps of memories. Victories and lingering battle wounds. We were two bodies that, while joined in the pursuit of life, still had our own edges. Separate yet really trying to be together.

Sitting there on the floor, I went through some of the old things we were storing. Photos from each of our childhoods and compact disc spindles piled high with ska music and Broadway soundtracks. Old college papers of mine, and some of hers that

I used to cheat from, littered the floor. Then, under a couple of books about addiction that had made the trip back from Seattle with me, I discovered a folder packed with newspaper clippings of theater reviews, press photos, and articles from my acting days.

I'd always believed myself to be a hopeful person, and it showed in the art I made. I took all kinds of risks. I created weird site-specific art. I auditioned relentlessly, constantly facing rejection, knowing that every no was one step closer to a yes. I traveled the country alone in my car, taking every theater job I could get. How was it that I could be so fearless in one aspect of my life but so fearful in another?

When I was twenty-three and barely out of college, the culture and arts paper in Indianapolis awarded me its annual Cultural Vision Award. I'd staged a performance art show based on an old Franz Kafka story in an alley, had been in several plays at my college, performed on most of the stages in the city, and had just finished a sold-out run in the title role of a rock musical called *Hedwig and the Angry Inch*. (Look it up. It's very odd and very amazing.)

In the paper is the following quote: "'You tell me I can't do something and I'm going to do it,' laughs Hogan, seemingly amazed by his own gumption, 'and it's going to be big.'"[1]

After a photo of me posing in my apartment from my first official press shoot, the article closes with this:

His choice of what some might consider risky projects are really vehicles that make it possible to connect with audiences in truly compelling ways. He's seen this happen when hundreds of people braved freezing temperatures to witness his adaptation of a Kafka parable over two nights in that Broad Ripple alley and again, triumphantly, during his extended run as Hedwig. "It gives you an incredible amount of satisfaction," Hogan reflects. "You reached people. And with that comes a sense of confidence."

He wants his art to change the world. "I'm 23 years old," he says, "just out of school. I still believe I can do that. And if not that, then what?"[2]

Oof. The thoughts of a self-perceived wunderkind hit me hard. While it's true that I had always been performing for one audience or another and thought rather highly of myself, I decided to let that kid off the hook for the hyperbole. Performing in front of an audience and making things kept me sane and kept me alive. Making art and being creative saved my life. But now I was on the edge of another kind of making entirely, and I couldn't seem to enter this new space with even an iota of the courage I'd had in this other world.

Past. Future. Present.

Marriage revealed how fuzzy I still sometimes felt as I stood in this blinding new light. I wanted to make good art and be a good human. I wanted to take risks in my art but also in my love. In the middle of the night, in the den lit only by the IKEA lamp Margaret had transported from her childhood room, I felt something new starting to make sense. The answer to the second question asked of Hagar, "Where are you going?" was still very much connected to where I had been.

Past. Future. Present.

I was so terrified that what had happened to me in the past—my abuse, my parents' broken marriage, the addictions my body used to salve my wounds—would repeat themselves in the future. And that fear of a fractured future, like that cursed tin woodsman, kept cutting me off at the knees.

But what if there was more? If I could think of life as a work of art, perhaps that would unlock something new. And maybe even more than *thinking* of something new, I needed to *imagine* it. Could I draw on my life as an artist? Could the hope I'd always had while making art *transfer*? What would it really look like to see my *life* as art? And what if I brought the same sense of daring and beauty into my actual life as I brought to the stage and screen? As I sat on the floor in our newlywed chaos of bins and boxes, I attempted to feel the energy and life bound up in the words: *radical imagination*.

What might happen if I chose to practice radical imagination for the sake of a better, alternative, and hopeful future like Margaret had written? I'd had years of practice doing it as an artist, but now I needed to do it in service of this new life I was trying to make.

25

Love Is a Net

Then I grasped the meaning of the greatest secret that human poetry and human thought and belief have to impart: The salvation of man is through love and in love.

Victor Frankl, *Man's Search for Meaning*

In Paris, the very first flight on the trapeze was attempted in 1859.

Connecting a short bar to two ropes, Jules Leotard took flight above his father's swimming pool. Soon after, the trapeze could be found in every major circus around the world, making Leotard a very famous man.

If you're wondering why his name sounds familiar, it's because the leotard we all know and love was named after him. It's what he always wore when he flew.

Even though I've been deathly afraid of heights for as long as I can remember, I also always wanted to try the trapeze.

It seemed dangerous and risky—things I naturally gravitated toward as a kid. If you're old enough, you might remember the '80s version of *Dancing with the Stars*, which was called *Circus of the Stars*. Same premise, but instead of celebrities dancing, they performed circus tricks.

In fact, one reason I wanted to be an actor was so I could be on that show. I figured it was the only way my mom would ever let me into the circus. Unfortunately, I never made it on the show, but a few years ago, for my birthday, my good friend Bjorn bought me a lesson and I finally got to try my hand on the flying trapeze.

As the instructor cinched my harness, attaching me to the safety wire overhead, I watched two other performers practice above me.

Swaying back and forth from his bar, the catcher dangling upside down yelled, "Listo!"

"Hep!" the flyer waiting on the board called back.

And with that, the flyer gripped her own bar, leaned back, and leaped into the air. Like two opposing pendulums, they met in the middle. Grabbing the flyer's ankles, the catcher called out, "Gotcha!" The flyer released her bar, and the two became one flying body arcing through the air. One more "Hep!" from the flyer triggered her release, and she fell gracefully into the net.

Then it was my turn.

Shaking a bit, I started up the ladder.

"Hi. I'm Jenny!" My cheerful instructor smiled, offering her hand when I finally made it all the way to the top. I calmed my breathing as she pulled me onto the platform. I had a good laugh to myself as I surveyed the ground twenty-five feet below. To delay the inevitable, I started making small talk.

"How'd you start flying? Is the weather different up here? Is it a law you all have to wear leotards? How ironclad is that release I signed?"

And then, offhandedly, I wondered aloud if fliers ever flew without a net.

"Hardly ever," Jenny said.

"But wouldn't that be more exciting?"

"It's the net that makes the risky stuff possible," she said.

The look on my face must have shown that I required further explanation.

"In a show, when someone is flying without a net, they are doing the most basic tricks. It looks scary to us, but to them it's old hat. It's boring. But when you have a net, that's when things get interesting."

And then, almost to herself, she said, "Yeah. Only an idiot would fly without a net."

For much of my life, I was that idiot. I wanted to do big tricks. I wanted to soar. I wanted to feel free. I was wild, and I wanted to fly without a net. I swore I'd never be married until I was at least forty. I didn't want kids. I didn't want a nine-to-five job. I didn't even want close friends. I didn't want to be tied down to anything.

Having a net of any kind had seemed a little bit like cheating to me. What's the risk if you know you're going to be caught? But this way of thinking had led me to a lot of falls and epic crashes, for a very long time. Broken promises. Broken relationships. Broken everything.

My friend's brother had just left his wife of only a year for a girl he'd been dating. He was teaching the girl's acting class, and they'd begun commiserating about their respective relationships over drinks afterward.

"What did you tell your brother, when he told you?" I asked my friend.

"I shook my head and told him he was so predictable. And I told him he was boring."

Boring. The ultimate blow to the artist. But my friend was right. His brother's actions were so predictable and oh, so boring. Nothing but the same old story we see played out over and over, again and again.

For a long time, I'd been the star of a major snooze fest myself.

During a marriage and family class in seminary, a professor helped me reframe this idea of risk and freedom. All this time I'd thought of relationships, marriages, and even close friendships as boring containers for accountability. Boundaries meant to wear me down and restrain me from being myself. When I told my professor this, he said something I've never forgotten: "I can understand your hesitancy, especially given your story. But, if you're willing to take the risk, take a real risk, it's in these very places where you will finally find freedom. Let's just hope you'll let yourself be captured enough by love."

As I jumped again and again off the trapeze platform, I realized something: the only way I had the courage to jump was because I knew the net was there. The only way I could leap into the air, out into the nothing, reaching for something I might not catch, was because I knew that if I fell, I would be caught.

And I was. Every time I tried and failed or panicked and let go, I fell into the net. Every time I stretched but couldn't quite make it, I fell into the net. Every time I tried something a little harder than I was ready for, I fell into the net. Caught. Shaken and breathless, but safe and held.

My thoughts went to a converstion I had with Dr. Lisa Miller, who studies the connection between science, the brain, and spirituality. She told me that when we are in an "awakened awareness," connected to love in the form of spirituality, we realize that we are loved, held, guided, and never alone.

It all started to come together.

If faith was a memory of the past, a memory of God's goodness and grace, and hope was a memory of God's goodness for the future, then maybe love could be the risky and daring container that would hold it all.

Maybe the net wasn't boring. Maybe the net was really the riskiest thing of all. Maybe the net was love. My instructor, Jenny, was right. So was my professor. And my friend. The net wasn't there to restrain me. It was there to set me free. Flying with a net didn't mean I was cheating. It meant I could commit to endless trying. It meant I could keep practicing. It meant I could even learn to soar.

Toward the end of my lesson, looking down at this massive web from the platform, I asked Jenny one more question. "How often do you have to replace these nets?"

Her answer surprised me again. "Oh, almost never."

"But don't they ever tear or get holes? What do you do then?"

"We repair it immediately. And actually," she added almost as an afterthought, "the places we do the repairs end up being the strongest."

Jenny!

I was stunned. This literally had never occurred to me. I'd always been quick to get rid of things that required mending or upkeep. If it was going to hold me back or take too much work, I left it behind and went on to the next thing. On to the next audition. The next job. The next project. The next person. I'd created a persona based on not missing out on what was to come. On fearlessly chasing what was next and new.

But in the end, I still missed out *and* I was boring.

I'd ripped and ruptured a terrible amount in my life, but when I thought it over, I realized I'd also done quite a bit of repair work over the last few years. Maybe I wasn't giving myself enough credit. Maybe I was stronger than I thought.

And I was never going to find the courage to jump if I always refused the net—if I always refused real love. Could I embrace the mutual commitment that made love possible? Could I be the kind of guy who sticks it out? Could I be captured by love?

That day my body was teaching me what my heart had been slower to figure out: love was a net, and it was time I let myself be caught. Leaping would not be easy. But I would have to keep trying.

"Hep!"

26

I Should Be
Philip Seymour Hoffman

On February 2, 2014, the prolific actor Philip Seymour Hoffman died of an accidental drug overdose in New York City.[1]

At the time, Margaret and I had been married a little over five years. Our first daughter, Ruby, was two, and our second daughter, Eloise, was only three months old. The net of love had officially enveloped me, and I was doing my best to keep jumping into its wide expanse.

After a series of moves to various apartments, we found ourselves living in my in-laws' basement as we worked to save a down payment for our first home. Hunting for ways to make extra cash, I'd started a side hustle by using all the creative lessons I'd learned over the last decade to create an online course called Make Better.

That night, Margaret had gotten Ruby to bed upstairs in

the room across the hall from her own childhood bedroom, while I'd coaxed Eloise to sleep in the storage closet behind the bathroom in the basement that had become her makeshift nursery. I'd just cozied up in our bed, which was jammed in the corner against the furnace room door, to nurse a nagging sinus infection and make a few last tweaks to the online course when the news alert about Philip Seymour Hoffman's death popped up on my screen.

This news rocked me. I felt a bit of my heart breaking. But not before it started to race with anxiety and fear. While I'd wanted to live Philip Seymour Hoffman's life, I now realized I came very close to dying his death.

Though our specific vices were different, we'd shared the same addiction of being unable to face the pain of the past or the fear of the future, and we'd numbed our bodies into submission by chasing the wind.

Philip Seymour Hoffman lost himself to the very thing he so desperately tried to loosen himself from, as he said in an interview on *60 Minutes*.

Hoffman says he doesn't drink and went into rehab at a fairly early age. "I got sober when I was 22 years old," he says. Asked if it was drugs, alcohol or both, Hoffman says, "It was all that stuff. Yeah. It was anything I could get my hands on. Yeah. Yeah. I liked it all." Why did he decide to stop?

"You get panicked. You get panicked," Hoffman said. "I was 22, and I got panicked for my life. It really was just that."

He said if he hadn't stopped it would have killed him and there were things he wanted to do.[2]

186

This made it even more devastating to learn of his death now. He'd wrestled his demons his whole life, yet they still got the best of him.

Philip Seymour Hoffman's life had inspired me. He made me want to be a better actor. But it was his death that reminded me that even genius, even money and fame, even decades of sobriety under your belt won't rescue you from the daily work of facing yourself just as you are.

That night, I wrote about Hoffman's death on my blog. I sent the post to Dan, who by now had become a mentor and a true friend. He and I shot missives back and forth, talking about the nature of hope and addiction.

He reminded me that every person who struggles with hope is an addict of some kind or another. And that addiction itself is a kind of madness. The thing that saved you from your emptiness so very long ago begins to kill you. And then, before you know it, it does. But before it kills your body, it attempts to destroy your hope. The madness we feel is because we've gone ahead and hoped for something new and different, Dan told me.

Frustrated, I declared my futility in a single-line email back.

Then why even hope?

His response was nearly instant.

Because while your addiction can kill you, it cannot kill hope. An addict, when they realize this glaring truth, must then wonder, "If I can't kill it, what would it be like to join it and let it spin me into something new? If it didn't kill me, and it cannot kill my hope, what if I let it set me free?"

And then, two minutes later, he added:

Oh! The other thing about addicts is that those of us who have survived aren't afraid of death. We can't be when we've stared that reality in the face every single day. And it's precisely this fact that makes the addict so terrifying in the face of evil. They can't *not* hope. Great post about Hoffman, by the way. What a tragic loss. Now go nurse that sinus infection and hug those ladies of yours!
—Dan

There's nothing like living in your in-laws' basement with a toddler, an infant sleeping in a bathroom closet, and an awful illness wracking your body to make you question hope. And yet I'd come too far. I'd jumped. The net really was made of love. Margaret and I were making good on our promise to *make*. But this business of imagining the future was so much harder than I realized and even more urgent. Because even though I'd thought I'd put my past in the rearview mirror, transmuting it into faithful fodder for the future, another old tale came creeping to the surface.

27

Learning Peace

For a year or two, I worked on writing a story about falling off a slide at a beach when I was four years old. Eventually I started fine-tuning it to tell onstage at church in a weekend service. I penned several drafts and finally, after putting it on the schedule, I set to memorizing it.

In my college acting classes, when it was your turn to perform a scene or monologue and it became apparent you didn't have the *whole thing* memorized, our acting teacher would send you home. She wasn't being cruel, she just wanted to be clear: "If you don't have your lines memorized, you can't tell the story."

She was trying to teach us what she knew: if you don't have your lines memorized, you can't be in relationship with your scene partner; you're simply waiting to hear a cue for your next line.

"Blah, blah, blah—"

My line.

"Blah, blah, blah—"

My line.

"This is not acting," she would say. She terrified me into taking memorization seriously, and it stayed with me.

A week into working on memorizing my story about falling off the slide, I started to feel a tinge of anxiety. It wasn't anything particularly acute but rather a slight increase in volume from the quiet rumble I still sometimes felt. I pressed on, but as the weekend approached, something happened that had never happened before.

I couldn't memorize my lines.

No matter what I tried, I couldn't do it. I'd get a few phrases in, and then my mind would jump to being in front of thousands of people, not knowing what to say, and with that terrifying picture whatever lines I'd committed to memory would be washed away in a sea of panic. To be fair, it had been a minute since I'd been onstage. But this was different. Something else was going on.

Saturday morning, I issued an SOS and asked if my lines could be put on the screen that sits just in front of the stage. The team obliged and I was saved. When the service finally came, I walked onstage, took a deep breath, and read my script.

I was four years old. Heat pressed against my tiny frame as I stood staring, neck craned upward, at a giant twelve-foot slide. The slide itself sat on a sandy beach near our house. I should note that it was one of those old-school, metal curvy things, with rusty, protruding screws.

This is not the kind of slide you'll find in a park these days with all its plastic and foam and safety regulations. This was an outlaw slide from the '80s—and I was going to make it to the top. The stairs led straight into the clouds, and up I went.

With one final heave, I pushed past the last rung and slung myself onto the sheet metal platform. I stood triumphantly surveying my imaginary minions below. I was the king of the Silver Lake slide! As I turned to head down the shiny curves, I reached for the thin rail that framed the platform but came up short. I tumbled off the twelve-foot ledge and slammed face-first into the sand below.

When I finally came to, I was stunned. I couldn't cry. I couldn't scream. And with every attempt I made at breathing, I drew in massive amounts of sand. Dry, gritty sand. All I wanted was a giant glass of water.

In fact, for weeks after the fall, I felt thirsty.

About halfway through my time working at the megachurch, I traveled to the Middle East on a trip with an organization devoted to understanding the peace process from all sides. One day, after traveling more than fifty miles into the sand dunes, we arrived at our final stop of the day. The moment I stepped off the bus and into the desert I was smacked with a wall of heat. The wind whipped up and a sandstorm swirled around us. In an instant, I was four years old again with my face in the sand. Gasping for air. Sand in my mouth. Dying of thirst.

After our adventure, which consisted of wandering through a valley tracing invisible borders dividing the land, our caravan loaded up and headed back to the city. Parched from the sand still scratching the back of my throat, I searched my backpack for water. Unable to find any, I closed my eyes and drifted into sleep.

By the time your body feels thirst, you're already dehydrated. And our hearts aren't so different: by the time our emotions catch up with our hearts, there's already something going on, drying us from the inside out. Bad doctor reports. Problems with teachers or bosses. That thing we just can't start doing. That thing we just can't stop doing. Our bodies tell us truths we haven't yet found the courage to utter.

It all takes a toll, and by the time we recognize we're thirsty, it can feel like it's too late.

Back in the bus, I was awakened by the sound of tiny pellets drumming against the tin roof of our bus. It took me a moment to get my bearings.

Rain.

The skies had opened, and it was raining. In the desert. In the most unlikely place, there was water. I laughed. The Holy Land knew.

As the bus rushed us through the storm, my mouth still gritty with sand, my friend Bjorn came walking down the aisle with a bottle of ice-cold water in his hand.

"Where did you get that?!" I nearly screamed.

"Oh, there's a cooler in the front of the bus."

Huh. I hadn't noticed.

It was raining in the desert and there was a cooler on the bus. I was struck with the notion that this image was somehow nudging me to recognize my courage. I thought of the rain and the bottled water—the refreshment that had been there all along. It made me wonder if the courage I'd been looking for all this time wasn't hidden in plain view as well. Perhaps my work was less about forcing something into fruition and more about opening up to something that was within me all along. Something neglected, but always present.

After the final church service on Sunday, I felt such a deep sense of relief. Thanks to the kindness and quickness of an extraordinary technical team, and some words writ large on a giant screen, the weekend went off without a hitch. I could put the story of the slide behind me. That night I fell asleep feeling so grateful that my anxiety had subsided. But two days later, *bam!* Full-on panic attack. I couldn't breathe. I couldn't focus. I hadn't felt this way in years, and I was scared.

I usually saw my therapist on Tuesdays, so luckily I had an appointment already on the books. I explained how I was feeling. And how I was confused that I'd had a panic attack after the weekend went so well. Even though I'd had such trouble memorizing my lines, everything had gone great. He was quiet and thoughtful. Then he asked me if I would be willing to retell the slide story. Although I was a little tired of hearing myself tell it, I obliged. As I got to the part where my little body slammed into the sand, my voice caught. It hit me: I hadn't told the whole story.

"What is it?" my counselor gently asked.

"I just sort of right now remembered. I wasn't alone on the beach. My dad was with me. And he had been drinking."

It all flooded back. That afternoon, the combination of summer sun beating against that metal slide and the demons floating in his vodka had gotten the best of my dad. With his judgment numbed, he'd allowed me to climb to the top of the slide without any supervision. It would've been a dangerous feat for a four-year-old even with an attentive adult standing by. But how much more perilous to be left to try alone.

As I sat in my therapist's office, the tears fell. I wept over not being caught by my dad. I wept for the ways he'd failed to catch me almost every time I needed him. For the ways our stories seemed so interconnected. But also I wept for the odd way my mind had neglected to remember that part of the story. There were plenty of snippets from other stories I'd told that I had left out. But those had been intentional, as I worried what people would think if they knew the whole truth. This was different. This was a detail that seemed to leave itself out as my subconscious mind attempted to protect me.

Until it didn't need to anymore. Until I was in a safe place with a safe person, ready for the whole truth, emboldened with the courage I hadn't known I already possessed.

———

Something else lingered from that trip to the Middle East. I'd encountered courage incarnate via a miracle of a woman named Robi Damelin. Robi emigrated from South Africa to Israel in the late '60s, creating a life she loved with two sons and her own advertising company.

On March 3, 2002, Robi answered a knock at her door to discover military officers who had come to bring her the news that her son David had been killed by a Palestinian sniper as he and his men crewed a checkpoint in the West Bank. Even as her heart shattered, she was explicitly clear to the officers who'd just delivered this tragic news: "You may not kill anyone in the name of my child." No revenge. No violent response. She had watched firsthand as destruction begat destruction and desired no part in it.

At first, Robi wanted to be left alone with her pain. But eventually she was persuaded to come to a gathering of bereaved Israeli families who could uniquely understand the dark tunnel into which she had fled. As they met, sitting in circles and sharing their pain, they took comfort knowing they were not alone. They realized there was a whole other group of devastated families like them—just over the border. And so, they made the courageous decision to travel to Gaza to meet Palestinians who had also lost family members in the conflict. This unlikely group became known as the Parents Circle, and today more than six hundred Israelis and Palestinians are members.

The power of meeting other mothers who had lost children was a transformative experience for Robi, and she came to understand that Israeli and Palestinian mothers shared the same pain over the loss of a child. This experience allowed her to know and feel kinship with bereaved Palestinian parents. Today she travels throughout Israel, the West Bank, and the rest of the world with a Palestinian partner by her side as they jointly share the message of the futility of revenge and the essential role courageous reconciliation and peacemaking must play in solving conflicts like the one that claimed the life of her son.

As we sat listening to Robi in the conference room of our hotel in Tel Aviv, utterly captivated, she told us, "To see the humanity of your enemy is the beginning of the end of conflict and the beginning of peace."

Robi offered us what she had learned through her personal tragedy, set against the backdrop of a generational, global conflict, and then she masterfully turned it right back to us with one powerful statement that has stayed with me ever since: "Where is *your* pain? Well . . . you'd better find it! Because that is where the good stuff is hiding."

I thought about my dad and the story I'd forgotten. And I thought about the work I might still need to do to find whatever good stuff was still hiding. The scale of my courage surely didn't come close to Robi's. But the heart of it beckoned. If Robi could find the ability to forgive from within the darkest tragedy her heart had ever known, then perhaps I could see the humanity in my dad and even in myself. I needed courage to see the humanity in my addictions—to see how waking up to them had truly saved me. And if I could make peace with myself, I wondered if I could make peace with my dad before it was too late.

28

Making Peace

A few weeks after my thirty-sixth birthday, I got another one of his calls. It sounded like the last few weeks had been rough on the old man. Another relentless Minnesota winter had sent him into a deep depression. He said the cold had gotten the best of him, and he couldn't take it anymore. He was drunk, calling from St. Joseph's Hospital in St. Paul. I stood on a corner in San Francisco as a fresh wave of deferred hope and devastation coursed through my body. For my birthday, Margaret had sent me out west for a weekend with Jarrod, who stood supportively beside me as I listened to my dad slur more self-contempt and apologies. Fed up with the cycle, I let my dad have it.

"I'm done, Dad. I can't do this anymore. I'm just . . . done."

February in San Francisco feels a lot like fall in the Midwest, especially around dusk. The light of the golden hour mixes with the crispy California winter air, and you'd swear you can smell apple cider and pumpkin spice. As Jarrod and I waited to pick up his wife from a church function, we walked around a bit, and I shared my mixed feelings of anger, sadness, and compassion I felt for my dad.

Before we knew it, we were on the steps of Grace Cathedral: stunning, gothic, sacred. We walked inside, both of us stopping to genuflect and make the obligatory sign of the cross beside the font filled with holy water.

Having grown up Catholic, I was used to cathedrals, but that doesn't mean I was immune to their power. Jarrod and I stepped quietly, heads cocked back to take in the 150-foot ceiling. And then we heard the music. Thinking it was canned at first, we followed the sound to the front of the cathedral and into a little alcove, where we discovered a small choir of nine or so women and men singing "Deep River" a capella.

The music echoed off the walls of the tiny room and then ricocheted out, filling the cavernous space we'd just walked through. I cried a bit to myself as we stood there. The room wasn't dissimilar to the one my dad had taken my brother and me to every week at The Church of the Epiphany. Every Wednesday, after delivering my brother and me to first communion class or youth group, he would put a dollar in the rusty metal donation box, light a candle, kneel, fold his hands, and beg to be released from his demons. Every single week he would ask God to fix all he had broken and to mend all that was broken inside of him.

After the choir finished, Jarrod and I explored more of the cathedral's beauty. We soon saw the choir members chitchatting with one another, exchanging the usual nonsense, like updates about children and what songs they should do next week. One man greeted his parents who were in from out of town. Something struck me about how ordinary it all was.

It was a lot like watching a show on Broadway that moved you to your core and then seeing one of the performers in plain clothes on the subway an hour later, reading the newspaper after a long day at the office. These singers, who had brought me to a higher place not fifteen minutes before, like they were angels, were just as ordinary as I was—which, of course, made me think of my dad.

Most kids want their dads to be superhuman. They want them to leap buildings and fly. But I don't remember ever thinking of my dad like this. For all his strengths as a charismatic salesman, the forces of darkness inside him always seemed to win, pinning him to the ground. More Clark Kent or Peter Parker than Superman or Spider-Man, my dad had always only been human.

And so I shouldn't have been surprised that his phone call had carried with it the sound of at least a fifth of vodka. His drunk calls have forever been more familiar than his sober ones. And yet I'd always held out hope that this time might be different. But, like the singers in the cathedral and the actor on the subway were just normal folks, my dad was not an angel, a superstar, or a superhero but rather a depressed, tragic soul with his own traumatic past, looking to feel just a moment of relief.

Before Jarrod and I left, we found a little nook filled with candles—some lit, some burned out, some just waxy puddles pooling around tiny flames. We both put a dollar in the rusty metal donation box and lit a candle.

I lit two.

About a block away from the cathedral, just as we reached the top of a hill, the sun still showing off its golden potential, Jarrod said quietly, "I lit my candle for your dad."

"Thanks," I said. "Me too."

My father-in-law, who also happens to be a recovering addict, says that to feel the pain of life means you're fully alive. To experience pain means that you're fully human. If that's true, and I believe that it is, then my dad is the most human person I know, which I've realized is something to be honored.

When you grow up with a dad who wrestles with addiction, you're always waiting for "the call." Has there been an accident? Is he back in rehab? Is he out of rehab? Has he died? When the musical *Hamilton* came out, I couldn't get this line out of my head: "I imagine death so much it feels more like a memory."[1]

When I first heard those words, I was so deeply grateful someone had finally been able to describe so accurately and poetically the deep rumbling I'd held in my gut for decades. When you live with someone whose addictive cycle seems neverending, you reflexively imagine the worst, if only to give yourself someplace to direct your underlying anxiety. Your heart is forced to do this strange gymnastic flip from being hopeful to being ready. You begin to imagine the worst when the worst becomes inevitable, which is when what you imagine starts to feel more like a memory.

I'd imagined my father's death so much that it did indeed feel more like a past event—how strange and surreal, then, when the memory finally came to pass. The call I'd been waiting for my whole life finally arrived. One day, while I was driving in to work, my brother left me a voicemail. When I called him back, his voice shook as he spoke.

"Um. Dad died."

I texted my coworkers, turned around and got back in the car, drove back home, and crawled into bed. There, in the stillness of the home Margaret and I had finally purchased with those extra funds I'd collected from my online course, I let the sadness lay on top of me like a weighted blanket I'd been waiting decades to use. And then I fell asleep for two days straight.

On the day of his funeral, I woke up early, brewed a cup of coffee, and sat at an old desk looking out the tenth-floor window of an old hotel in downtown St. Paul. I imagined I was Garrison Keillor penning his latest episode of "The News from Lake Wobegon." But instead I was writing the eulogy I was to deliver later that morning. As I pulled together the last couple phrases, it started to snow. *Dad would've hated this weather*, I thought—and decided that should be exactly how I would start.

After the most moving rendition of "Deep River" I'd ever heard (inspired by the choir in San Francisco), and then a solid tribute from my brother in full Marine dress blues, I stepped up to the plate, looked out at a mishmash of family and friends, and began.

My dad hated this weather. Vehemently despised it. And as he was a man who never wore underwear, I can understand why. The cold wind just blows right through you. So, in a way, I'm glad he passed before real winter hit. But then again, I'm not. I don't think any of us are. And yet, there may be some among us who are relieved. Of which I am that as well.

Such is the nature of living with someone who suffers from the illness of addiction—you get good at living in the tension.

And so, for the time that remains, I want to give tribute to the glorious tension that was my dad's life.

A couple of months ago, when it seemed like death was rapidly approaching, Margaret and I made the trip up from Chicago to see him at a nursing home. My dad and I hadn't spoken in some time. When I walked into his room, the old man was, in fact, an old man. White beard. Oxygen mask. Sweatpants baggier than usual. Still no underwear.

He struggled to his feet, and when he was finally upright, we hugged. His once strong, now bony arms wrapped around me and my wife. He held on for dear life. Which, when we were alone, is what I thanked him for.

Dear life.

I told him I was grateful for the life he had given me, the breath he'd given me. For without it, I wouldn't be a dad to my daughters, Ruby and Eloise.

As the late August sun glared off the golf game playing on the TV in the background, we spoke of the usual father/son, end-of-life stuff. How he taught me how to ice skate but could never get me to stop on my left side. Even the rink I built in our backyard when I was fourteen was of no use. How he taught me how to use wit and charm to obtain deals and discounts. And while I learned, retained, and have even used many of his techniques over the years, watching my dad trying to negotiate with the seventeen-year-old host in hammer pants for better seats for the *Aladdin* show at Disneyland will always go down as one of my top ten most embarrassing moments. We talked about how I struck out in the ninth inning in my fourth grade baseball tournament, ultimately dashing our hopes for a championship. And how, in the front seat of his car, through coffee and cigarette breath, he said it was OK if sports weren't my thing. We spoke of my daughters, of Margaret, of the garden I'd started, and of my work. We spoke of the regrets he still held, and I did my best to let him know he was off the hook.

And finally, we spoke of the pride he held in my brother and me. The kind of deep pride someone extols when they see their kids doing something they could never do.

For those of you who followed along in Sunday school, the fifth commandment is to "honor thy mother and thy father." The Hebrew word for "honor" is *kabode*, which literally means "heavy" or "weighty," and that's exactly what this feels like right now. It feels heavy and weighty to give honor to a man I didn't fully know.

In his novel *Godric*, Frederick Buechner describes the moment when the main character loses his estranged father. The character says this: "The sadness was I'd lost a father I had never fully found. It's like a tune that ends before you've heard it out. Your whole life through you search to catch the strain, and seek the face you've lost in strangers' faces."[2] I think I'll spend my whole life straining my ears to catch the song my dad sung and squinting my eyes to locate the shadowy figure that entered and exited our lives so frequently.

And yet, despite his very human flaws, I believe my dad was made in the image of God. This is what I loved about him most. This is what we all loved about him most. I know that he reflected the absolute goodness and grace and beauty of the God whose likeness he was fashioned in. The tragedy, of course, was that he never believed it.

Which is why I'm so grateful to be standing here looking at all of you. I have the distinct honor of standing before the embodiment of my dad's goodness and grace and beauty. The *imago Dei* that you reflected to him his entire life now fills this very room. And the face I struggled to find my entire life is found now in your faces, the faces of all the people who loved him. Thank you for showing him such great care when it seemed he couldn't care less.

When my dad held Ruby for the very first time, he remarked how peaceful she looked as she slept. It's a standard phrase grandpas say. But for him, it was different. Something else hung in the air as he held my sleeping newborn. It was longing. Longing for peace. For himself.

And now that he has shuffled off his mortal coil and the flesh that so easily entangles, I know that he can no longer deny his goodness, his grace, his beauty. And I know he is finally at peace.

I returned to my seat, and Margaret reached for my hand. I closed my eyes and thought back just two months, to the last time I'd seen him and the words we'd exchanged. I exhaled. In that moment, on a bitter morning in November in a crowded funeral home, I was at peace as well.

29

Practicing Peace

We found out we were expecting our third daughter several months after my dad passed. All this circle of life stuff was surreal. Though I was still working through waves of grief, it was time to let go of the hope I'd held, even during my long periods of estrangement with my dad, for change. There was nothing left to hope for. His story had ended. But mine had not. He was gone, but I was still here, hunting for ways to unlearn the songs he taught me or at least transpose them into something new. And so even months after his death, I kept returning to our final conversation, set in a quaint and kindly nursing home, hoping to find more gold and a little more peace.

An old story goes that, as night set in, a rabbi took a wrong turn on his way home. Eventually, he found himself at the foot of an enormous castle. As he stood before the door, shivering in the cold, a guard yelled down from above.

"Who are you, and what are you doing here?"

"Say that again!" the rabbi called back.

The guard repeated, "Who are you, and what are you doing here?"

"How much do they pay you?" the rabbi snapped in return.

Wondering what the rabbi was driving at, the guard told him his wages. Without skipping a beat, the rabbi replied, "I will double your salary if you stand outside my door and ask me those two questions every morning for the rest of my life."

Who are you? What are you doing here?

These weren't questions about names and places.

These were questions about identity and purpose.

When Margaret and I made the decision to go see my dad that last time, we were nervous. We drove through the vast sea of Midwestern cornfields, wondering if this might be the last time we'd see him alive. I contemplated a father who warred against the rabbi's questions. He couldn't stick with the discomfort that came before real peace. Those questions seemed to pit him against himself, exposing a war expressed through alcoholism, addiction, apathy, and depression.

His ongoing battle hijacked his entire life. As a result, our relationship struggled and at times was nonexistent. I longed for a dad who could live peacefully in his own skin and in his unique purpose—who knew who he was and what he was doing here.

How do you prepare for a conversation like this one? Margaret and I weren't sure. But we did our best. We tried to stay focused on what we wanted to communicate. To keep our expectations low. And to remember that we were not making this trip to receive but to offer—not to hear healing words but to speak them, if only to ourselves. Although, to be honest, I am not sure these two adult children of alcoholic parents could help but have a smidge of optimism that maybe, *JustDearGod-PleaseJustMaybe*, this would be the conversation that would save everyone. Even still, our focus was to give words of peace.

It was a beautiful afternoon. My father was happy, if not a little apprehensive to see us. With Margaret bearing witness, he and I both did our best to reach across the expanse between us. Eventually, Margaret left us alone to pace and pray in the garden courtyard below, holding hope for something good to make its way through, for the peace that had eluded us for so long.

We sat side by side, making small talk with tears in our eyes. Two adult men not sure what to hope for. A father and a son. It didn't take long for his words to turn to his failures and regrets and shame. The long list of things he wished he had done differently or not done at all. I tried to listen with compassion. And then, as truthfully as I could, I offered him my forgiveness. I didn't pretend he was a good father. I didn't pretend the things he'd done or the things he'd failed to do didn't affect me. Instead, I named the ways they did. I named the harm they caused. And that the boundary I'd recently set between us was not to punish him. It was to protect myself, my young family, and my own sobriety. I tried to tell him who I was and how intimately I had known some of his struggles— more than he'd ever know.

Finally, I told him that even though he'd fought his own goodness his whole life, he could be at peace—if only he'd give in to grace. But, of course, I'd named the impasse. I knew it almost as well as he did. He was stuck in his story and stuck in his past, and because of it he was unable to imagine a new and different future that might have allowed him to finally live a different life in the here and now.

While I did my best to set him free, he just wouldn't give up his shame. He was determined to hold on to it to the bitter end. And so, I had to do the worst thing a codependent person can do: *nothing*. I had to simply sit with it. No fixing. No forcing. No convincing. No saving. I had to let the man have his shame, because I was no longer going to hold it with him.

When I was in my twenties, I thought having a dad like mine was a perfect excuse to avoid answering those two big questions the rabbi paid for. Why not make a mess of my own life and blame it on what I'd been handed? In so many ways, his cycle catalyzed mine.

But then I got into recovery and tried to stop hiding. I got married and tried to stop hiding a little bit more. Then, in what proved to be the absolute kicker, I had daughters. And as it turns out, you cannot hide from daughters.

In the end, even though he had not been ready or willing to give in to grace, I was. Even if his addiction falsely threatened him, mine hadn't killed me—and, more importantly, it hadn't killed my hope. In our conversation that August afternoon, as I offered freedom through my forgiveness, I granted myself some too. Because that day, while I attempted to set him free, I also freed myself.

Before I left, I showed him some pictures of our daughters. As I watched my dad swipe through the images of these girls whom he'd never have the privilege of knowing, I was overcome—overcome with the desire to leave them good gifts, not heavy burdens. I didn't want my daughters to carry the weight of a dad who spent his life at war with himself, at war with the world, at war with God. I knew how that felt. And so did he.

One of the greatest regrets my father carried to his grave was that he never made peace with his own father. His dad was a violent alcoholic who took out his anger on his son through near-weekly beatings. My dad spoke of this often. Mostly when he called me while drunk. Through vodka-laced tears, he'd share the deep worry he held that he hadn't broken the cycle and instead passed along his inability to forgive his father (and himself) to me.

In English, the word *peace* can often conjure up a passive picture—someone free of strife and conflict—but in Hebrew, the word for "peace," *shalom*, means something very different. It means to be complete, to be whole. And so, if I could forge some deep sense of who I was and what I was doing here, if I could cultivate a sense of peace and forgive my father, perhaps I could move toward wholeness. And maybe I could extend forward to the next generation what I had not been able to extend back to my father, nor he to me.

The Great Minnesota Get Together, also known as the State Fair, was in full swing the weekend Margaret and I visited my dad. After such a heavy afternoon in the nursing home, we treated ourselves to baskets of hot, salty French fries, buckets of warm cookies from Sweet Martha's Cookie Jar, and ice-cold lager from the beer garden. Margaret had never been to the fair, and I took personal pride in sharing some of my nostalgic childhood with her. As the sun set, we boarded one of the gondolas that take you up and over the grounds. Looking down at the landmarks I'd wandered through with my dad as a kid, I snuggled Margaret close for a selfie. And as I snapped a picture of our stuffed, sunburned faces, words from poet Rainer Maria Rilke came to mind: "Be patient toward all that is unsolved in your heart and try to love the *questions themselves*. . . . Perhaps you will then gradually, without noticing it, live along some distant day into the answer."[1]

Perhaps one of the greatest gifts we can give to our children and to those closest to us is to make peace with who we are and what it is we're doing here. *So, who am I?* I'm a husband, a dad, a friend, a maker, and a unique reflection of a mysterious and good God. *What am I doing here?* I'm making. Building. Confessing. Unlearning. Relearning. Re-membering. Loving. Turning toward home again and again. Forever and ever. I am receiving grace. And I am learning to make peace.

30

Breaking Promises

How do you muster peace when it's all falling apart?

Ten years working at the church went by quickly. And at the same time, ten years working for the church felt more like forty. The grueling schedule of creating something new every single week at such an enormous scale took its toll. But in a million ways, it was worth it. It had become a colossal net of love in which to fall again and again, personally and professionally. It was where I created so many incredible friendships, most especially with another young filmmaker named Bjorn. Like Margaret, Bjorn was a true ally in the making, and we often joked that we were "creative life partners." Bjorn taught me to see light in new ways, and he taught me to push boundaries. He helped me to find my deep inner artist, and also to know when it might be time to leave. He left the staff himself two years before I had the courage to.

While my brother needed to join the Marines to learn about discipline and consequences and accountability and how to grow up, I'd needed to join a church staff to learn adulting. I'll spare you my hilarious and insightful commentary on the similarities between the geopolitical/military/religious complexes in which we both found ourselves for another time.

But yes, in so many ways, it was worth it. Until it wasn't.

Like a child who has outgrown her parents' home, I longed for spaces where I could be more myself, where more of me was desired—maybe even where *all* of me was desired. But large, successful institutions don't necessarily become large and successful because their people are running around just being themselves. No, too often they become what they become because of who they tell their people they can be.

Freedom begets freedom. And because I'd found so much freedom in my heart and soul after nearly fifteen years of recovery work, I was ready for even more. I no longer wanted to be quiet about certain beliefs. I no longer wanted to be tied to unyielding loyalties. I wanted to work where I could be part of creating culture and not merely co-opting it for the sake of attracting people into the fold. On top of that, I was dismayed by the fact that the institution at times looked like it was more interested in protecting itself than its people.

Margaret and I knew it was time to begin my exit. With another baby on the way, we decided I'd stay employed until our third child was born. Our daughter burst quickly into life, three weeks early, on a Sunday in September. She was ready to join us and showed so little concern about timing that we barely made it to the hospital on time. We named her Nora Jade Josephine. Since she completed our trilogy of daughters, we gave her all the middle names we'd kept in our back pocket.

Even as she slept peacefully in my arms, life around us began to shift. The ground began to shake. Everything we knew about family and friends and community started to come undone.

As my time on staff wound down, the rumblings around the church turned to tremors, and the cracks in the foundation began to grow. Reports of inappropriate behavior by our pastor, abuses of power, and years of cover-ups and hoodwinking came to light. We watched as people we loved were unable or unwilling to tell the truth. And then factions formed. Friendships split. Meetings were called that hosted more PR people than pastors.

That's when I realized I'd been here before. The room our staff rallied in to hear the latest news and plan the church's strategy of denial was the same room I'd sat in all those years ago when I learned I hadn't been the only one of Ed's victims. I couldn't help but see how it was all connected. We were told to listen to our leaders and not to those accusing them of harm. And then, instead of hearing them weep for the women affected, I watched as they cried for themselves. "Why would those people want to ruin his reputation?" they condemned. "What do they really want from all this press!?" they accused. "What's a 'gold standard' investigation, anyway?" they gaslit.

Margaret and I were heartsick. The place we knew and loved—our jobs, our family, our community, and the center of everything we'd come to know and love—was ripping apart at the seams. And then the exodus happened. One by one, families uprooted and moved away. Staff member after staff member quit. In the subsequent year, many more were eventually let go. On two different snowy days, we saw off two different

213

families—our closest and dearest friends. Both had made us one of their last stops before they left.

No longer speaking to each other, one family drove west and the other east, leaving Margaret and me standing somewhere in the messy middle of it all. It was too much to take. What followed was the painful work of untangling our hearts from the place, the leaders, the dynamics, and the relationships we'd grown accustomed to. We could no longer hold the secrets and silencing loyalties. We hoped there was still good work to be done at that church, but we knew that work was no longer ours.

The pandemic hit a year and a half after it all broke apart, after I'd officially left my job at the church to make a go at becoming a film and commercial director. We lost a lot of money from work that was postponed or canceled, we lost friends to the virus, and friends lost family. For a season, it was all very scary. But we did our best to stay hopeful as we hunkered down and waited and did all the online school with our girls. During quarantine I started taking an online course offered by poet David Whyte.

For years, I'd wanted to engage in his in-person experience, where he guides groups around Ireland, speaks his poetry over them as they journey, and asks them all along the way to contemplate what it means to be human. Of course, when the entire world shut down, this was not to be. And so he turned his attention to Zoom and asked those interested to virtually join him in doing everything he'd have done while traipsing through hill and dale in the Irish rain from the quarantined comfort of our very own homes.

These weekly Sunday sessions became a lifeline for me as directing work dried up and the lockdown took its hold. A coincidence not lost on me was the fact that David was delivering these mini sermons from his home library on Bainbridge Island—a mere mile or two from the exact spot my time in the Pacific Northwest had ended at Dan Allender's recovery week nearly thirteen years prior.

One Sunday, David spoke of promises. Not ones that needed to be kept or even remade but the ones that needed to be broken. He began by reciting one of his poems.

To Break a Promise

Make a place of prayer, no fuss,
just lean into the white brilliance
and say what you needed to say
all along, nothing too much, words
as simple and as yours and as heard
as the bird song above your head
or the river running gently beside you.

Let your words join
one another
the way stone nestles on stone,
the way water just leaves
and goes out to sea,
the way your promise
breathes and belongs
with every other promise
the world has ever made.

Now, leave them go on,
let your words
carry their own life
without you, let the promise
go with the river.

Have faith. Walk away.[1]

To read a David Whyte poem, while stunning, is nothing compared to hearing him read it. His lilting mix of Irish and Yorkshire accents trills a touch as he recites his own verses, not reading them straight through but pausing often to repeat a word or even an entire line half a dozen times. He is not a man afraid to take his time. Slowly, as you listen, you drop into a meditative state as his everyday *lectio divina* takes hold—his words becoming waves and wind that carry and call you deeper into the text.

Make a place of prayer, no fuss,
Make a place of prayer, no fuss, no fuss, no fuss
just lean into the white brilliance

On and on he went. Week after week after week. The pandemic pressed on. Sunday mornings, for me, became like that tether Midwestern farmers tied around their waists to get to the barn and back safely. The one I'd tied to myself back in Seattle had been left with its other end dangling in the breeze, but now I had a home I could anchor it to, both figuratively and literally, even though the idea of it was about to be put to the test.

So many people from our core community had gone. Margaret and I realized it was time for us to leave our neighborhood too. Who knew we'd be the last ones standing? I'd already left staff, but we had continued to attend the church. Until now. It was time to leave. Time to leave the church within walking distance. The church that had created the most stunning vision for a community I'd ever been a part of. The church in which I began recovery. The church that let me keep on recovering. The church where Margaret and I fell in love while attending and serving. The church where we were married. And the church that had crumbled before our very eyes, turning friends into foes and scattering the people we loved across the country.

The place loomed large in all the ways. From the corner of our bedroom, where I clung to the lilting lines of David Whyte's missiles of hope from Bainbridge Island, I could see the tip-top edge of the roof of this church that had given and taken so much.

We needed to break some unhealthy promises we'd made to that place, to our community, even to our own families. We had to do what the last line of David's poem says.

Have faith. Walk away.

31

Destination Unknown

"OK, great! I'll just put you down as 'Destination Unknown.'"

That's what Chad from PODS told me after he asked where we'd like our storage containers shipped to. When this stranger so casually named our existential crisis, I literally laughed out loud.

For some time now, we'd known we were ready for something new. An adventure. A place to rest and heal. A place we could all thrive. And so, we waited. To be pushed or pulled. Called or compelled. As we sat in that liminal space, Margaret did that thing you really should never do, at least not in the middle of a global pandemic, civil reckoning and unrest, and e-learning during an election year. She prayed something like, "God, if we are supposed to move, You're going to have to bring someone to our door literally asking to buy this house."

And, well, God did what God sometimes does in those situations and showed off, because that's exactly what happened. Our house was not on the market when friends of friends called us, asking if we wanted to sell our house. We did. *To them?* Yes.

Now, most people sell their house because they know where they are going. They have a job they are moving for or are moving to be closer to family, or perhaps they simply love the ocean, city, mountains, fill-in-the-blank, and can't imagine not living in that locale. But the only thing we knew was that we needed something new. *Where?* Who could say? *When?* Right now!

And so, with some cash from the sale of our home, we decided to take our show on the road and go on an adventure of living out of furnished rentals until we found the right place for us to put down roots.

"Bridges" by Johnnyswim played on repeat as we began to pack. This song essentially became our own anthem, our cry to burn the old bridges in search of new adventures. About halfway through the chorus, they sneak in this little line: "The love that we keep is the shelter we find."[1]

Before we left Chicago, I hired a designer to create a Hogan family logo. We wanted something that looked like a mix between a collegiate flag and a boutique furniture store logo. Something simple. Black, with big bold letters that simply read Home Team.

Once we'd settled on our design, I had large decals printed. I put one on our minivan as we prepared for our trek and saved the others to put up on the windows and doors of all the places we'd go. The logo was a reminder to us all that home wasn't a place but rather people. *Us.* And the love we'd made as this family of five was the shelter we'd always be in, no matter where, no matter what.

32

On Ambivalence

If you are a professional director, eventually you'll come to a place in your career where you sign with a production company. In essence, they become your manager, and they represent you and your work, which is (nearly) exclusively with them and their team. The next step after this is often joining the Director's Guild of America, the union for professional directors, where all the big girls and boys making movies, TV shows, documentaries, and Super Bowl ads convene.

Attaching yourself to a production company and joining the union are big moves and not to be taken lightly. And while there's no clear path for any director, there are familiar processes along the way. Because of the kind of work I was doing, I was both comfortable and confident that I'd most likely stay a freelance, non-union director for some time. Lower budgets. Always selling my work. The only one selling my work.

I'd gotten calls over the years from various production companies with offers to sign, but I'd never felt like I was in the right place or they were the right people. Signing on to a company exclusively can sometimes mean having to turn down work from other companies. It would be like having a full-time job working at a Ford dealership while also working on the weekends for the Toyota dealership across the street. There can be a conflict of interest. I'd always harbored the fear of what I might be leaving behind were I to sign on.

Yet I also longed for a team. A place to belong. A company filled with people trying to do good in the world with the gifts they've been given. I dreamed of what it might feel like to not be the only one looking for work. To know someone else was out there fighting on my behalf.

Before leaving the church, I took close to two years to build up a freelance career so that when we eventually left, we'd be jumping into something already in motion. Much of that freelance work came from the unceremonious and often humiliating work of cold-calling and emailing. I'd scour the internet for the emails of executive producers, heads of production, agencies, and reps, and then I'd just hit them up.

Sometimes I had interesting work to share, and I'd lead with that in the subject: "New Director + New Work with LeBron James and Usher. :-)"

Sometimes I just tried to be interesting: "What if I worked for you for free?"

My rate of return hovered around 2 percent. It wasn't pretty. But knowing it was a numbers game, I kept a visual tab of my attempts by writing the name of the person or company I'd contacted on a square of paper and then stabbing that square onto an old-fashioned diner receipt holder. That way I could see that even if I wasn't getting traction, I was making progress. (At present the spike holds maybe one thousand "tries.")

Eventually enough "tries" would pay off. Eventually the numbers would tip in my favor as enough of those calls turned into enough relationships and then . . . eventually . . . enough jobs. Work. Gainful employment making things.

And then, every month, I'd start over. The number went back to zero and I'd get back to it. Sometimes I'd be lucky enough to have strung a few things back-to-back, or I'd done a good enough job on one project to be invited back for more. But at the end of the day, our little business was going to survive only if I kept doing the hard work of trying to find more work.

One day, I received a call from a production company offering to sign me exclusive. While certainly exciting, it also left a ball of stress knotted in my stomach. I was a forty-one-year-old man with a family, and the offer stirred up a tremendous number of questions, hesitations, and ambivalence.

Their offer seemed good, and the team being created comprised a diverse mix of amazing directors. The company had been started by three women with a focus on true diversity, equity, and representation. They were doing meaningful work in good, meaningful ways.

Perhaps, if I signed, the work coming my way would be more interesting, the budgets would be a bit bigger, I'd have a team of people helping to develop me along the way, and maybe, just maybe, I'd no longer be the only one looking for work on my behalf. Still, I wasn't sure.

"So, why all the ambivalence?" Margaret asked as we sat on the couch. "Stop. And close your eyes," she instructed.

I knew what she was doing, and I wasn't having it. I opened my eyes wider and stared back, daring her to continue. Which, of course, she did.

"Close your eyes and take a deep breath," she said.

Begrudgingly, I obeyed and tried to get in a couple of deep breaths.

"What are you afraid of?" she asked slowly.

"I'm not afraid!" I shouted back and opened my eyes.

"Then what is your ambivalence?"

Margaret was using story work against me. For the last few years, she had been seeing a therapist who trained under Dan Allender. She was even participating in a story group much like the practicum groups I'd been part of in Seattle. I'm not always great with vocabulary, so I asked in the snarkiest of ways, "And how would you *define* ambivalence?"

She returned my snark with a smile and continued, "It's where your goodness, your desire, and your hope have been met with harm."

Ouch. She didn't stop there.

"I hear you saying all the reasons this could be good. But I'm watching you get stuck for all the reasons it could turn," she said, and paused for a long moment. "This is just like when your dad promised to move your family out of that old house, out of that old neighborhood. So many promises for good. They all came back empty. Same thing with the car he planned to buy you. Only to disappear. *Of course*, you are afraid to hope. You're still the little boy who had to figure it out alone, who got punished for trusting. But the longing wasn't wrong. The wishing didn't make you bad. And people not taking care of you when they should have had nothing to do with you."

And there it was. I'd still been so scared to hope, to truly lean into my desire, because my story had too often reminded me that I would ultimately be met with harm. Margaret was right. I was afraid of what I couldn't control. What if I said yes, but it didn't work out? What if I agreed to give it a try, but I ended up feeling tricked? What if I thought I was saying yes to something good, but it turned out to be bad? I desperately wanted to avoid feeling foolish or embarrassed. And beyond that, what if I said yes, locked myself in, and there was no work? What if the jobs never came?

But perhaps the worst of all my ruminations was this: What if I said yes and the other shoe *didn't* drop? What if things did work out? When you've lived a life of constantly waiting for the calamity you know will inevitably come, the idea of things going well can sometimes be the scariest of all.

It was time for a dose of my own medicine—for another shot of past, future, present. It was time again to dive into hope. Could I believe that this step toward something I truly wanted could lead to good for me and for others? Could I believe that even if things didn't end up going how we'd planned, that we'd all still be OK?

My wife reminded me that there were no guarantees. Certainly, this was a risk for me and our family, and it was possible we'd be proven wrong in the end. But she also reminded me that we weren't helpless kids anymore. Our radar for dangerous people and dangerous situations had vastly improved, as had our ability to listen and act on that radar. Also, I'd continued to find the goodness of my past, which kept slowly freeing me to imagine a new future. And on a practical note, we had some money saved up. We also had the ability to have brave conversations with the company about our concerns. We could negotiate terms that felt right and good for us.

And even if we failed, we would survive. This was something we hadn't always believed was true. But here we were, standing in the ruins of the greatest collapse we'd known in our adult lives—still breathing, still alive, and still hopeful, if a bit trepidatious, on the verge of something new.

In the end, I decided not to let my past persuade me that there was no use in hoping for a different future, and I moved ahead with defiant courage and found my yes.

And yes is what Margaret and I just kept saying.

33

Family Motto

Our family logo and the adventure on which we were about to embark were undergirded by a family motto Margaret and I had been developing over the years. Our marriage rallying cries all revolved around making, to which we remained committed. But with three girls now in the mix, it seemed like something new might be in order. We wanted a few words or short phrases that would act as a shorthand between the members of our little family and could be used to encourage, embolden, and remind our daughters who they were as part of this family. Because, like us, they are human and tend to forget.

The summer before the pandemic, I took Ruby to her very first volleyball camp. Volleyball made sense for her. She's tall. Athletic. Oh, and her uncle TJ was a collegiate volleyball superstar. She'd been watching him from the sidelines for years, including winning a division championship and making a run in the NCAA tournament. She was elated when TJ offered to give her a lesson in volleyball basics before her camp started. They practiced bumping, setting, and spiking in our driveway. He was kind and playful and encouraging. She was so proud and very excited.

But when we walked into the enormous high school gym on that first day of the camp, I could feel her freeze up. It was clear she was going to be the youngest of the bunch as we followed the crowd of extremely long legs and ponytails. Most of the parents dropped their girls off and went along their merry way. Sensing Ruby's unease, I stayed and sat on the bleachers with her while we waited for the camp to begin.

I took my phone out and snapped a photo of our girl to send to Margaret, and I noticed Ruby was biting her tiny lower lip ever so slightly. Her eyes were big and looked like they might give way to tears. She seemed so little—because, I think, she *felt* so little. I bent over and gave her a hug, reassuring her that it was going to be awesome. That *she* was going to be awesome. As I held her close, I could feel her heart beating out of her chest. I bent closer, looked her in the eyes, and whispered what have since become our Hogan Family Rules:

Be kind.
Have courage.
Fail.
Ask for help.

These phrases had emerged and evolved over time. The first two copy those uttered as a final decree from the ailing lips of Cinderella's mother to her heartbroken daughter in the 2015 live-action version of the film. Somehow, they stuck with us. We repeated them to each other regularly. We wanted the girls to approach their lives, their stories, their sisters, and themselves with kindness. To approach the world as though it was meant to be good. And we desperately wanted our girls to have courage. To feel within themselves a sense of power and resilience, to recognize their inherent largeness.

Our next rule was from a talk I heard from the founder of Spanx, Sara Blakely. When asked how she connected becoming such a successful entrepreneur to her family, she simply explained that her dad had encouraged her to fail. She went on to say a common question from her dad around the dinner table each night was, "How did you fail today?"[1] Rather than her being afraid of making mistakes, he wanted her to be comfortable with the idea of failure, to lean into it, even to go in search of it. Following suit, we began asking our girls that question at the dinner table. "I tried to answer the bonus question but got it wrong." "I went up to the new kid to say hi, but I think he was shy and he ignored me." Whatever failure they brought to the table, we celebrated it.

And then we added our last rule, "Ask for help," because we didn't want our daughters to get stuck in the unhelpful lie that asking for help was bad, weak, or made someone a burden. We didn't want them getting locked in their heads or bodies, carrying around unnecessary cargo. We wanted them to know that in this family, we ask for help when we need it. Which is why they know we see counselors. They know we have a money coach and a business coach. They see the books we are reading about parenting and recovery and our nervous systems and how to build a business. They know the friends we call when we hit a wall, emotionally or professionally. Because we all need help. And we wanted our girls to see the good that comes from asking for help. Margaret even started reminding our oldest two that there are no badges in our house for suffering silently.

Ruby's fear that day was so real I could almost grab onto it. But I couldn't take it from her. And I couldn't talk her out of it. I did the only real thing I could. I sat with her while she was afraid. I didn't make her wait alone. As I sat quietly by her side, I got to thinking.

Fear. I'm not sure it ever goes away. In that season, there was plenty to be fearful of. The last couple of years had pummeled us. Suddenly, the coaches' whistles began calling players to attention and I began to wonder if fearless people really existed. Or, rather, if "fearless" people were simply scared people who kept moving forward anyway.

So, at that very moment, I added a fifth line of motivational prose to our list, and the one that became the mantra of our household in this tumultuous season:

Hogans do it afraid.

Whispering in Ruby's ear, I recited our motto. "Be kind. Have courage. Fail. Ask for help. Hogans do it afraid."

She loosened her lip, quietly nodded to herself, and waded out into the sea of eager girls. As I left, she caught my eye and gave me a thumbs-up. I returned the gesture and tried with all my might not to fall to the floor weeping in a puddle of fatherly pride.

Every time I'm scared, which is often, I try to remember that thumbs-up. Ruby's sweet signal across the gym wasn't screaming, "I'm going to CRUSH this!" Instead, she was saying, "I'm going to do this. I'm terrified. I'm small and inexperienced and know nobody. But I'm sticking it out. I'm staying. Because I want to try. I'm going to do it afraid."

What a gift. To stay soft and present in a world set up to make you callous and cold.

She stayed. Then she went back the next day. And the next. She loved it. And she learned even in the moments when her knees are wobbly and her heart is racing, she can find herself. She can be kind. She can have courage. She can fail and ask for help. She can do it afraid.

And if she can, so can I.

One of the miracles of parenting is that if you're paying attention, sometimes you get to reparent a broken part of yourself. Or, crazier yet, your own offspring casually repeats something back to you, giving you something you didn't realize you needed.

As we packed up our house, one of the last things to go into storage was the little white desk in our bedroom. It had become holy ground for my weekly sessions with David Whyte. I'd needed my Zoom tabernacle with this poet and his wisdom until the very last minute. One week, near the end of our time in Chicago, he shared a poem called "The Seven Streams." A handful of lines called out, arresting me. I leaned back in my chair, listening to David twirl the words he'd written into sweet refrains of truth that seemed to keep me afloat.

Through the window, I noticed our neighbor. He'd had knee surgery just before lockdown. For weeks he could barely move, hobbling with every step, the pain heavy on his face. But no matter the weather or the discomfort, he'd kept moving. Walking. Healing. Now he was jogging. I'd gotten into the habit of timing my daily walk down the driveway to the mailbox around the time he might pass by. I'd shout, "I'm so inspired!" He'd smile and wave back, probably more invested in the podcast playing in his headphones than anything I had to say. But as I watched him round the corner that day, I hoped some of his fighting spirit would rub off on me. The packing and preparing had me tired. I was scared and unsure I had it in me to take this next big step into the unknown.

Just then, David's voice broke through:

> Be a provenance of something gathered,
> a summation of previous intuitions,
> let your vulnerabilities
> walking on the cracked sliding limestone
> be this time, not a weakness, but a faculty
> for understanding what's about to happen.[2]

Each Zoom session ended with a Q&A. That day, a man about my age, with dread in his voice, asked a question about his children. Scared of the stress that these "unprecedented times" were causing him, he wondered if it would trickle down and ruin his young daughters, whom he'd been so hard on lately. With tears in his eyes, he wondered if they would be all right after all this.

Instead of answering the man's question, David told us a story. When he became a father to his boy, he said, he felt like he knew what to do. What to say. How to guide his son on a path of goodness and truth. David was hoping to correct any mistakes his father had made with him, and would try to do it all one click better with his son. But a daughter ... oh, a daughter was very different. With his daughter—for him, at least—came a realization that he hadn't the facilities to teach her in the same way as his son. He might not be able to teach her at all. Instead, perhaps what he needed was to learn from her. He finished the story by simply saying, "I needed to apprentice myself to my daughter."

Then David circled around to answer the man's question more directly. With reassurance grounding his voice, he said that he believed the man's children would be all right, and that instead of worrying he wasn't teaching them what they needed to know in this season, maybe he could consider if there was something he needed to learn from them.

"But if you're asking for my advice, tell them this: 'All your intuitions are true.' That might be the most powerful thing you can ever tell your children."

Our middle daughter, Eloise, is like a tiny prophet. She sees the world in her own way, which means she catches things other people miss. She asks questions about the things people are not saying. In lots of ways, she *knows*. Like mother, like daughter. But with less filter than her mother has, she goes right ahead and says it.

Eloise was playing on the kitchen floor as I shared with Margaret how nervous I was feeling about our move. There were so many big waves of emotions. I felt so vulnerable, yet I couldn't wait. Excitement bubbled underneath the fear. Oh, ambivalence! A few minutes later, as I grabbed my keys to head to the hardware store for another batch of packing supplies, Eloise stopped me.

In her flannel nightgown, she pulled me down and whispered: "Be strong. Be brave. Don't be nervous. Don't be scared. Have happiness inside you."

I was speechless for a moment, and I hugged her tight. Then David's blessing to children tumbled out as I held my tiny apprentice. "Lulu, all of your intuitions are right. Thank you," I simply said.

"My what?" she asked.

She was seven.

"Your hunches, your gut."

"My heart?"

"Yes. Your heart."

Her little voice of truth tickling my ear was just the reminder I needed. And my words back to her were just the words the scared little boy inside me needed as well. The words we use matter. They shape the stories we tell. Eloise's words, reaching me from a mess of curls and freckles in an Elsa nightgown, lifted me and reminded me of the story we were trying to tell with this family—and reminded me that all my intuitions were right. I headed out to get the last of the supplies we needed for our move.

34

Free People Free People

The time is ripe for looking back over the day, the week, the year, and trying to figure out where we have come from and where we are going . . . to enter that still room within us all where the past lives on as a part of the present, where the dead are alive again, where we are most alive ourselves to turnings and to where our journeys have brought us. The name of the room is Remember.

Frederick Buechner

Sometimes I hear people imply that the past is better left in the past. No reason to dredge up what has come and gone. I used to think that too. Diving into the past meant I was trying to hold on to it, or maybe I wasn't enlightened enough to let go of it. I also thought that talking about old pain would only bring new problems, which was the last thing I wanted.

But I discovered that getting stuck in a loop of rehashing isn't the same as doing the work of re-membering. And simply endeavoring to forget something doesn't erase it or its impact. Refusing to name that which has formed us only gives those shadows more power. We end up controlled by silent forces we can't grasp, doing things we don't understand.

Had I not been willing to change my relationship to my story, it most certainly would have killed me. And I couldn't have freed myself from the clutches of a past that was trying to dictate my future until I had the courage to face it. It is in these most tender places of brokenness and through these harrowing memories of tragedy—as we stand by the river like Hagar, out of breath, clenching our fists, hoping that no one sees the darkness within—that El Roi, the God who sees, quietly waits for our response to His two questions.

Where have you come from?

Where are you going?

The secret is that when we invite a good and curious God, along with a trustworthy community and sometimes a skilled therapist, to redeem the stories clenched within our fists, our creativity truly comes to life. Our transformed relationship to an old past helps us to imagine a new future. And imagining a new future allows us to live differently today. I'm not sure I can call this creative act anything other than *grace*.

As Frederick Buechner says, the work of remembering, then, isn't looking back but rather looking *out* as you enter a room to do the unthinkable. To do the thing they say cannot be done. It is entering a room in which the shadows of your past playing on the wall are renamed, redeemed, and re-membered into something entirely new.

It was while I was in that space that I felt God kept asking me, *Will you trust that new life can be found in the ruins? Will you stop hiding in the shadows of old stories so you can be seen? Will you tell the truth so you can be free?*

And then the question of all questions came, careening from the cave, sprinting through the forest and the fog, ricocheting off the riverbed, reverberating with holiness as it landed softly on the tear-soaked shores of Puget Sound: *Will you tell your story so you can change your story?*

As I tried and trusted, then tried and trusted some more, I found there was new life even amid so many little deaths. Because I changed my past and because I've been seen, this amazing grace has gifted me the freedom to see differently. I've realized that the greatest art project of my life *is* my life; I now understand that, in the end, this new way of seeing, this new understanding of creativity, is what ultimately *saved* my life.

However, I must confess there's something I haven't told you. There is more to the story of the cave. A twist.

After the man has struggled to emerge from the darkness, pulling himself through the muck and mire, after the smarting subsides and he's gotten used to the light, he does the unthinkable. Instead of picking up and running as far and as fast from the cave as he can . . . the man returns.

Back into the dark he goes.

Stumbling to find his friends, who are still stuck staring up at the shadows, he has a message to declare. An anthem beating in his heart. He returns to the start of his own journey, his cry resounding off the dank, dark walls as he shouts, "There is more! So much more!"

With eyes now accustomed to light, it is disorienting to squint back into the void. But he is compelled. His discovery demands action. The man doesn't let the fear of where he'd been deter him. After all, he found a way out, a way that led him to the kind of beauty that overwhelms. The kind of revelation you can't keep to yourself.

I knew, then, that I had to go back too. To tell my story of where I'd been and where I was going.

Isn't this all any of us who have found a modicum of freedom are trying to do? Isn't this what recovery groups are for? And sponsors? And therapists and honest small groups? And long tables and comfy couches? And humans who don't give up on you, or who have the guts to let you go until you finally give up on doing it your own way?

Isn't this what theaters and concert halls are for? And books and films and music and art that shake you to the core with the truth: the universal is almost always found in the particular?

Isn't this the power of someone telling you their tale? When you hear the stories of people who have been to rock bottom and back, who refuse to leave you behind, and who are willing to show you the way? In the tales of people who share their stories and show you their scars? In the humanity of those who pray for your courage, who sit with you till the urge to use or hide or numb passes and you can breathe again? Who, with the humility of a prodigal, share all that they have learned? That's how I made it: other people did the work and then didn't keep it to themselves.

Do you think the man, returning to the cave, was well received? As he shouted promises of a reality that seemed impossible, do you think those casting the shadows or those chained and entranced were happy to see him? They were not. They were angry and suspicious. As people sometimes are when you invite them back to life.

I am glad I didn't think about this along the way. The possibility of extending any goodness I received wasn't on my radar for a long time. I was just trying to survive. I didn't work this hard or come this far to reenter the cave. I didn't escape to freedom only to return to the darkness of my captivity.

But you know what? I didn't work this hard and come this far to not go back either. What good does it do to untangle yourself but then leave others in bondage? What is the point of finding a life outside the cave if you can't invite others to come along? In other words, free people free people.

This is what I said to that conference audience as I stood onstage the morning after they'd all seen me nearly naked. As I shared the particulars of my own story in my own way, I wanted them to know that no matter what dark cave they found themselves in, I knew something of their struggles. They were seen. Where they'd come from didn't need to define where they were going. And, if they wanted, there was a dot of hope waiting for them whenever they were ready.

I told them as long as I live, I will offer to anyone who will listen the truth-filled anthem beating in my heart:

There is more. There is so much more.

Epilogue

Four Straight Lines

For years, decades really, I told myself I'd never get a tattoo. As an actor, I couldn't imagine marking this perfectly clean canvas. I needed to be able to inhabit whatever character I was asked to play and simply couldn't fathom messing up the blank slate.

But after we had Nora, something started to shift. The role I inhabited at present was of husband and dad, and I started wondering if maybe my tune was changing. Instead of being afraid of messing up a blank slate for a role to come, maybe I should mark the one I was actually playing now.

And so, I labored—for years—over what tattoo I might get. And then one day, just a few months ago, it hit me: four perfectly straight lines. One for each miraculous lady.

My wife and my daughters have invited me into a life I didn't know I could lead. They tell me the truth. They let me be silly. They love me in a way I still have to stretch to grasp. And there is no place I can go that they don't go with me. This felt like the right thing at the right time.

After all these years, Jarrod has remained my best friend, and when he came to town to visit, it was just the push I needed to take the leap. As we approached the tattoo place, I noticed a man sitting outside, staring out into the distance, obviously high.

"I hope that's not my guy," I joked to my buddy as we sauntered in. I could feel my heart racing, but I was resolved.

Inside, it was a laidback and cool vibe. We made our way to the front desk and waited for someone to help us.

"Four perfectly straight lines," I told the owner when he finally introduced himself.

After some paperwork and a Venmo transfer, I was in the chair. And guess who wandered in to do my tattoo? Yes. The man who had been sitting outside. I was already nervous, but now I was unsettled. I made big eyes at my friend, unsure what to do. I took a deep breath and tried to stave off what felt like panic. But I was here, I was ready, and who could mess up four perfectly straight lines?

That night, my panic *mode* turned into a panic *attack* as I rolled around in bed, staring like an obsessed maniac at my arm. My brand-new tattoo was covered with ointment and a clear bandage. The skin was scabbing, and I just couldn't see for sure. But deep down I knew. Those four lines, now permanently on the inside of my forearm, were NOT perfectly straight!

I felt trapped and mad and panicked and foolish. I should have waited. I should have been clearer. I should have asked for someone else to do the tattoo. But it was too late.

The next morning the girls couldn't wait to see my new ink. I was way less excited than they were. I tried to muster energy and a positive tone as I revealed the still-bandaged tattoo, introducing them to each individual line that represented each one of them. There was much squealing and jumping. They were effusive and barraged me with a zillion questions about the experience. Was I afraid? Did it hurt? Did I cry? How long did it take? Could I still play in the pool? What did I *mean* I couldn't play in the pool? How long till I *could* play in the pool?

I told them the story. And then I confessed how disappointed I was because the lines were supposed to be perfectly straight and they were not as crisp, narrow, or perfect as I wanted. And now I was stuck with imperfection on my arm. I told them I was wondering about trying to get the lines fixed, hoping there was some way I could alter them into what I wanted. I lifted my chin, ready for the refrain of sympathy and care.

I was not prepared for the outcry of indignation. Ruby and Eloise went *off*, interrupting each other, to let me hear it.

Ruby started, "Dad! Why would you want those lines to be perfect?"

Eloise launched in, "Yeah, Dad. We're not perfect. We'll never be perfect. Nobody—"

"Dad, those lines are supposed to be us. But you wanted them perfectly straight? You tell us perfect is boring—" Ruby interrupted.

"And we don't want to be boring!" Eloise added. "You always say we can be different and strange and not the same. Why would you want perfectly straight lines?"

Margaret smiled. "So, you don't think Dad should try to get those lines to be perfect, then?"

Collective outrage: "NO!!"

241

Eloise summarized it simply: "We are bumpy and curvy and squiggly, and we aren't perfect, Dad. The lines shouldn't be perfectly straight."

Apprentice yourself to your daughters, David said.

I was stunned. But I shouldn't have been. These girls have no problem shouting truths I am still trying to embody. Thankfully, they are fearless teachers. They merely showed up, fully themselves, and held up a big mirror to their old man. They invited me back to myself.

As the months have passed, these four imperfectly straight lines have grown on me. As have all the lines that have marked me. Each reminds me to meet my life as it is. To meet myself as I am, not who I was. To remember that the practice of courage, creativity, and radical imagination is just that: *practice*. And that the goal of practice is never perfection. No, the goal of practice is *progress*, and progress will always be messy. Never up and to the right but rather a constant spiral of forward motion followed by setbacks, losses, grief, and death—and then life, always life, something my story refuses to let me forget.

Acknowledgments

The fact that this page of acknowledgments even exists is a miracle. Mainly because it means I finished my darn manuscript! I signed the contract to write this book in 2018, and, of course, at the time, I had no idea what it would take to tell my story—silly me. And while I'm listed as the author, there is a literal army of incredible humans to thank. Because, if not for them, there would be no book. And to be honest, if not for them, there might not even be a me.

Margaret, your faithful support of this work—the book and the project of my life—is unmatchable. You read, wrote, and edited passages without end. This book is better because of you, and so am I. I'm forever grateful for your desire to continue to make together no matter the odds or the costs.

Ruby, Eloise, and Nora, it's true what they say, you cannot hide from daughters. Thank you for seeing me and letting me see you.

Dan, since I know you relish hyperbole, suffice it to say that this book would not have come to pass without The Seattle

School, its faculty, students, and most importantly, you. Your life is a gift to me that I will never be able to thank you for properly.

Jarrod, from Wii tennis elbow injuries to business ventures to simply the most remarkable friendship of my life—you helped me whiteboard, spreadsheet, edit, and talk this book into existence.

Steve and Sarah, you have been through it with us, and I'm grateful for all that we've shared and will continue to share. Thank you for being the best cheerleaders, early readers, and believers in these ideas.

Bjorn, my creative life partner—though we didn't make this one together, your voice encouraged me throughout.

Cyndi, thank you for holding my pages with such care and attention when I desperately needed someone to do so.

Rob and the Nugs of Beverly Hills, while I implemented approximately zero percent of your suggestions, you gave me something far greater: the courage to keep going.

Alex and the Bindery team, thanks for your unending confidence that I had something to say and your endless patience as I figured out how exactly to say it.

To "Writing Coach Meredith," as you were lovingly referred to in our home for many months. Thank you for your grace, persistence, and presence as you helped me work the words out of my body and onto the page.

To Rachel, for taking a chance on this idea. You were the one person in the field that got it, and for that, I am eternally grateful.

To Stephanie and the team at Baker, for the endurance you

mustered as I chipped away at these ideas and stories, and for the constant encouragement to keep going "bird by bird."

Blake, who would have thought we'd end up down the street from each other in this season of life as I finished writing this book? So very grateful for you and your family.

And finally, to Mom and Dad, for life, dear life.

Notes

Introduction

1. Ronald Rolheiser, *Forgotten among the Lilies: Learning to Live beyond Our Fears* (New York: Doubleday, 2004), 3.

Chapter 2 Waking Up

1. Mayo Clinic Staff, "Panic Attacks and Panic Disorder," Mayo Clinic, May 4, 2018, https://www.mayoclinic.org/diseases-conditions/panic-attacks/symptoms-causes/syc-20376021.

Chapter 8 Now or Never

1. Ben Sherlock, "20 Best Quotes from the Jurassic Park Franchise," Screen Rant, November 12, 2021, https://screenrant.com/memorable-quotes-jurassic-park-franchise/.

2. Dan Allender, *The Wounded Heart: Hope for Adult Victims of Childhood Sexual Abuse*, rev. ed. (Colorado Springs: NavPress, 2008), 159, emphasis in original.

3. Allender, *The Wounded Heart*, 19, emphasis in original.

4. Robert McKee, *Story: Substance, Structure, Style, and the Principles of Screenwriting* (New York: Regan Books, 1997), 200.

Chapter 16 Hiding and Being Seen

1. Laura Merzig Fabrycky, "God Is Not Elsewhere: Poetry, Prophecy, and Sight," The Washington Institute for Faith, Vocation, and Culture,

accessed March 1, 2022, https://washingtoninst.org/god-is-not-elsewhere
-poetry-prophecy-and-sight/, emphasis in original.

Chapter 19 Golden Possibility

1. Peter Block, *Community: The Structure of Belonging*, 2nd ed. (Oakland:
Berrett-Koehler Publishers, 2018), 16.

Chapter 20 Seeing the Light

1. Plato, *The Synposium*, trans. Christopher Gill (New York: Penguin
Books, 1999).

Chapter 24 Past. Future. Present.

1. David Hoppe, "Blaine Hogan," NUVO, July 7, 2003, https://nuvo
.newsnirvana.com/culturalvisionawards/blaine-hogan/article_d577547e
-6316-11e7-a845-7b255073e62e.html.

2. Hoppe, "Blaine Hogan."

Chapter 26 I Should Be Philip Seymour Hoffman

1. Portions of this chapter adapted from Blaine Hogan, "I Should Be
Philip Seymour Hoffman," Blaine Hogan, accessed March 10, 2022, http://
blainehogan.com/articles/i-should-be-philip-seymour-hoffman.

2. Daniel Schorn, "Philip Seymour Hoffman Gets Candid," CBS News,
February 16, 2006, https://www.cbsnews.com/news/philip-seymour
-hoffman-gets-candid/.

Chapter 28 Making Peace

1. "My Shot," MP3 audio, Lin-Manuel Miranda, on *Hamilton: An American Musical*, Atlantic Records, 2015.

2. Frederick Buechner, *Godric: A Novel* (New York: HarperSan-
Francisco, 1999), 51.

Chapter 29 Practicing Peace

1. Rainer Maria Rilke, *Letters to a Young Poet*, rev. ed., trans. M. D. Herter
Norton (repr., New York: Norton, 2004), 27.

Chapter 30 Breaking Promises

1. David Whyte, "To Break a Promise," *The Sea in You: Twenty Poems of
Requited and Unrequited Love* (Langley, WA: Many Rivers Press, 2016), 56.

Chapter 31 Destination Unknown

1. "Bridges," MP3 audio, Johnnyswim, on *Moonlight*, BMG Rights Management, 2019.

Chapter 33 Family Motto

1. Emma Fierberg and Alana Kakoyiannis, "Learning to Celebrate Failure at a Young Age Led to This Billionaire's Success," *Business Insider*, June 17, 2018, https://www.businessinsider.com/sara-blakely-spanx-ceo-offers-advice-redefine-failure-retail-2016-7.

2. David Whyte, "The Seven Streams," *River Flow* (Langley, WA: Many Rivers Press, 2007).

Blaine Hogan is a writer, film and creative director, and actor. Formerly the creative director for Willow Creek Community Church, Hogan is currently a full-time filmmaker. He lives in Atlanta, Georgia, with his wife, Margaret, and their three daughters. He holds a master's degree in theology and culture from the Seattle School for Theology and Psychology and has appeared in many stage productions and television shows. Find him online at www.blainehogan.com.

CONNECT WITH
BLAINE

Journey together with Blaine to grow your creativity and courage.

———————————————— FIND HIM ONLINE ————————————————

f Blaine Hogan   **◎** BlaineHogan   **🐦** BlaineHogan

BLAINEHOGAN.COM

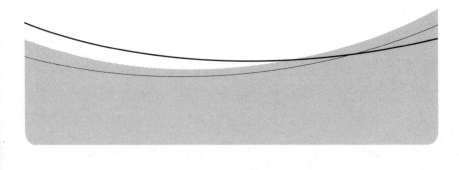